Progressivism: A Very Short Introduction

Very Short Introductions available now:

For more information visit our web site
www.oup.com/vsi/

Walter Nugent

PROGRESSIVISM

A Very Short Introduction

OXFORD
UNIVERSITY PRESS

OXFORD

UNIVERSITY PRESS

Oxford University Press, Inc., publishes works that further
Oxford University's objective of excellence
in research, scholarship, and education.

Oxford   New York
Auckland   Cape Town   Dar es Salaam   Hong Kong   Karachi
Kuala Lumpur   Madrid   Melbourne   Mexico City   Nairobi
New Delhi   Shanghai   Taipei   Toronto

With offices in
Argentina   Austria   Brazil   Chile   Czech Republic   France   Greece
Guatemala   Hungary   Italy   Japan   Poland   Portugal   Singapore
South Korea   Switzerland   Thailand   Turkey   Ukraine   Vietnam

Copyright © 2010 by Oxford University Press, Inc.

Published by Oxford University Press, Inc.
198 Madison Avenue, New York, NY 10016

www.oup.com

Oxford is a registered trademark of Oxford University Press.

Library of Congress Cataloging-in-Publication Data
Nugent, Walter T. K.
Progressivism : a very short introduction / Walter Nugent.
p.   cm.
Includes bibliographical references and index.
ISBN 978-0-19-531106-8 (pbk.)
1. United States—Politics and government—1865–1933.
2. Progressivism (United States politics)—History—19th century.
3. Progressivism (United States politics)—History—20th century.   I. Title.
E661.N84 2010   324.2732'7—dc22   2009025810

9   8

Printed in Great Britain
by Ashford Colour Press Ltd., Gosport, Hants.
on acid-free paper

For Bernard A. Weisberger
True Friend and Lifelong Progressive

Acknowledgments

I would like to thank Scott Rook of the Oregon Historical Society, Lisa Marine of the Wisconsin Historical Society, Mary-Jo Miller of the Nebraska State Historical Society, and the staff of the Prints and Photographs Division and the Photoduplication Service of the Library of Congress for locating, providing, and granting permission to use images from their collections.

Many helpful suggestions have come from Oxford's readers of the manuscript—Robert D. Johnston, Tom Dorrance, and one anonymous. Bernard A. Weisberger, historian and friend for decades, and Suellen Hoy read the entire manuscript and offered many comments; how I have used them is of course my responsibility.

My editor at Oxford, the tireless Susan Ferber, has been unfailingly prompt and helpful at every turn.

Contents

List of illustrations

Introduction

In the history of American society and politics, "Progressivism" was a many-sided reform movement that emerged in the final years of the nineteenth century, flourished from about 1900 to 1920, and faded away by the early 1920s. In national politics, its greatest achievements occurred between 1910 and 1917. In state and local politics and in private reform efforts—churches, settlement houses, campaigns to fight diseases, for example—Progressive changes began appearing in the 1890s and continued into the 1920s. In these social-justice efforts, legions of activist women, despite lacking the suffrage, were enormously effective. Most prominent in national politics were the "big four": William Jennings Bryan, Theodore Roosevelt, Robert M. La Follette, and Woodrow Wilson. Mayors Tom Johnson and Sam "Golden Rule" Jones in Ohio led change in their cities, as did governors Hiram Johnson of California and James Vardaman of Mississippi. Lincoln Steffens, Ida Tarbell, and the rest of the crusaders (known as "muckrakers") spearheaded what would later be called investigative journalism. Progressive educators ranged from university presidents to philosophers to sociologists. In philanthropy, Chicago's Julius Rosenwald supported Booker T. Washington's Tuskegee Institute, while the Rockefeller Foundation poured millions into education and health in the South. The Baptist Walter Rauschenbusch, the Episcopalian W. D. P. Bliss, and the Catholic John A. Ryan led their churches toward social justice, and by 1910 every major

Protestant denomination espoused what was called the Social Gospel. A major progressive-era innovation, the settlement house, combated poverty, ignorance, disease, and injustice in many cities, led outstandingly by Jane Addams and Ellen Gates Starr in Chicago, Lillian Wald and Florence Kelley in New York, and Mary Workman in Los Angeles.

Successful reform movements need followers as well as leaders. Progressivism had millions of followers across the country, electing legislators who put Progressive statutes on the books from Massachusetts to Kansas to California. Some Progressives pushed only one or two reforms, while others called for a broad spectrum. By the time the movement played itself out, many of these objectives had been achieved, particularly those intended to reduce some of the inequities—iniquities, a Progressive would likely have said—and problems that had festered and spread from the unregulated capitalist economy that developed after the Civil War ended in 1865.

Progressivism reflected a growing, if temporary, consensus among Americans that major changes in the late nineteenth century had produced unwelcome, un-American imbalances in their society. Evidences of this were a new class of ostentatious millionaires, monopolistic and out-of-control corporations, conflict (often violent) between workers and capitalists, and supine responses from governments. A traditional suspicion of cities intensified as many middle-sized ones proliferated and a few immense ones expanded, fed not only by migrants from the American countryside itself but also from unfamiliar parts of Europe and Asia. Cities seemed to produce social ills—poverty, prostitution, disease, drunkenness, despair—not that the countryside, especially in the South, was free of such things. But cities, especially large ones, drew more attention.

What could or should be done about all this? How could governments be made more responsive to "the people?" How could economic life be made fair again? How could American society remain faithful to its long-held core values, yet cope with new forces?

Progressives tried in many ways to answer these questions. Most of them favored using some form and degree of government—local, state, or federal—to regulate economic problems, ameliorate social ills, and reconcile change with tradition. Such willingness to use governments broke with the anti-regulatory attitude of the "Gilded Age" that preceded the Progressive era. By 1919 America had changed in many particulars, with a lot of social problems solved (especially for the small-town, small-city, white middle class), though others had hardly been touched. Yet the sense of crisis so urgent in 1900 had passed, whether from the many reforms themselves, from war-weariness, or from a sense of expanded individual opportunity. When all was said and done—despite its incomplete and inadequate attacks on society's problems—the Progressive era constituted one of the longest periods in American history when reform was generally welcome.

Because Progressivism manifested itself in everything from railroad regulation to woman suffrage to immigration control to realist art and literature to the first real mass media and paved roads, the movement's core theme has been hard to pin down. "Reform" itself was that theme, vague as the term was and is. But much of the Progressive spirit lay in that very openness to change, that conviction that "something needs to be done." How, when, and by whom those changes were carried out is the concern of this book.

The consistent conviction of virtually all Progressives was that a "public interest" or "common good" really existed. Margaret Thatcher, Ronald Reagan, and conservatives of similar mind have denied that there are such things, and, as Reagan famously said, government itself was the problem, not the solution. The result in the post-Reagan years has been legislation and political ideology that is radically individualistic, and certainly not conservative in the traditional philosophic sense. In short, the history of those years played out on a different premise than the Progressives'. Whether we like the individualistic or the societal view better, we can study these century-past reformers to understand that there once was a different consensus.

Not every American of the early twentieth century became a Progressive. As always, some people resisted change in all things, while for others almost no reform went far enough. For the mass in the middle, however, change was desirable and necessary. This mass comprised the followers of the Progressive movement, without whom leaders like Bryan and Theodore Roosevelt would have accomplished little. Both leaders and followers were essential. By 1920 progress had indeed been made on many fronts; American society had moved a long way from where it was in 1900. Yet not everything changed; some backsliding happened in the conservative 1920s, yet overall the main contours of America persisted. At root, Progressivism was reformist, not radical.

Progressivism was a movement of many concerns. It included a wide range of persons and groups, and it arose in different versions in every region of the country. It crossed the lines of party, class, gender, and even race. In the industrializing and urbanizing Northeast and Midwest, Progressives fought against corruption and cronyism in city and state government, and repression of workers in factories and mines; they also fought for public education, clean cities, and responsive governments. In the predominantly agrarian South and Great Plains, Progressives fought against railroad monopolies, scarce credit, exploitation of child labor, and chronic diseases. In many states they promoted woman suffrage. In the exotic and underpopulated Far West, they sought all of these things. On great national issues, such as tariffs on imports (before 1915 the chief source of federal revenue) or imperialism, they divided—Republican Progressives advocated higher tariffs as Republicans always had, and they usually favored aggressive expansion, while Democratic Progressives sought lower tariffs and opposed such colonialism as the annexation of the Philippines in 1898. Eventually, by the second decade of the 1900s, most of them agreed on broad measures such as the graduated income tax, the direct election of U.S. senators, and woman suffrage, though not always on the details. The majority also supported two policies that were not part of the liberalism of the New Deal and later, immigration restriction and prohibition of alcoholic beverages. The majority of Americans in the early twentieth century, Progressives included, did not believe in racial equality; those were the peak years of segregation, Jim Crow laws, and lynchings. Yet some Progressives joined to create the NAACP and the Urban League. No one favored American imperialism more than Theodore Roosevelt, yet he was undeniably a Progressive leader. Many favored entering World War I against Germany, yet Jane Addams, William Jennings Bryan, and many other Progressives opposed it strongly.

In sum, there were many varieties of Progressivism and Progressives. They held in common, however, a conviction that society should be fair to its members (white native-born ones, anyway), and that governments had to represent "the people" and to regulate "the interests." It went without saying that there was such a thing as "society." The progressive "big four"—Bryan, Theodore Roosevelt, La Follette, and Wilson—and the many less visible Progressives for all their differences shared a belief in society, a common good, and social justice, and that society could be changed into a better place.

Chapter 1

The predicament: the discontents of the Gilded Age

Why did Progressivism happen when it did, rather than earlier or later? Why were enough Americans "ready for reform" by 1900 and willing for the next fifteen to twenty years to make it happen?

Progressivism began emerging in the closing years of the 1800s, developed with accumulating speed from about 1900 to 1917, and then fragmented and faded during and right after World War I, from 1917 to the early 1920s. Why then? Briefly, because Americans increasingly gained the sense, as the nineteenth century lumbered through its final years, that their society was changing—sometimes for the better, but in important ways, for the worse. Undoubtedly better were the prosperity that marked the 1880s, the multiplication of miles of railroad tracks that promoted and enabled economic development, the first electrified city streets and public places, and the first skyscrapers. On the other hand, undoubtedly worse were the working conditions in factories and mines, the monopolistic control that those very railroads placed on millions of farmers, and above all the increasingly visible disparities in rewards between the most fortunate members of society and the general mass of people. The rich were getting richer—far richer—than most people. Up to a point that seemed reasonable and justifiable, but beyond that point, it felt unfair and unjust. What, if anything, could be done?

Rumblings of discontent were apparent as early as 1880. For some decades before that, Americans very often thought of society as a harmonious collection of people engaged in producing and distributing things. Farmers produced grain, cotton, and livestock; skilled craftsmen built houses and shod horses; manufacturers produced nails and rails; shopkeepers sold them. The economy consisted of small producers. Hardly anybody was extremely rich or extremely poor—and shouldn't be. Nonproducers were suspect, sometimes called manipulators of the wealth that real people produced. Reality did not always match this ideal, but the harmonious association of producers and the very secondary role of nonproducers was how American society should be. The best American political economist of the nineteenth century, Henry C. Carey of Philadelphia, theorized that the good society consisted of the harmonious association of its members. The act of production was vital and honorable. The great French observer of the United States, Alexis de Tocqueville, visiting in 1831, explained that Americans loved change, but they hated revolution—because they were a people of "scanty fortunes," none really rich, but all with some property to invest, nurture, and defend. To these writers, American society succeeded, not because its members were equal but because opportunity was widespread, and property was, in general, fairly distributed.

The profound unfairness that American society wreaked on its nonwhite members was foreign to the theory of Carey or the observations of Tocqueville. The immense fracture of the recent Civil War and subsequent Reconstruction belied talk of harmonious association, given that over 600,000 had died in that war and that deep sectional and racial hostility persisted long afterward. Nonetheless, the ideal of harmony, and the democratic, wide dispersal of economic and political power that permitted and supported it, continued to satisfy a great many Americans as an answer to the question, what should America be like? Producerism was optimistic, rosy-eyed, and to some extent mythical, yet it did seem to define how the political economy of the country worked.

That country, as of the late 1870s, looked like this: Just under 50,000,000 people were scattered across 3,000,000 square miles of land between the Pacific and the Atlantic. About a third of them lived in the Midwest, another third in the South, two in seven in the Northeast, and fewer than one in twenty-five in the vast West. More than 43,000,000 were white. Fewer than 7,000,000 were African American, of whom over 90 percent lived in the South. Thirteen percent were born in other places, led by Germany, Ireland, Canada, Britain, and Scandinavia, in that order. The only nonwhite minorities, other than blacks, were about 100,000 Chinese (nearly all in West Coast cities or railroad stops) and perhaps 400,000 American Indians, also living mainly in the West. In short, the majority of the population was homogeneous, white, and native-born, but it also included sizeable minorities of blacks in the South, Asians and Indians in the West, and immigrants in eastern and midwestern cities.

What did they do? They farmed, more than anything else. Sometime during the 1870s those who worked on farms began to be outnumbered by those who did other work, but not by any single kind. The nonfarmers divided mainly among factory workers, service workers, professionals, business people, and commercial workers. Americans had always been a farming people, and the majority continued, until about 1920, to live on farms, or in small villages even if they worked at something other than the land and livestock. Many people who did not actually farm were, nonetheless, agrarians. They shod horses, made barbed wire, ran country stores, and preached in country churches. Furthermore, many of those who no longer lived on farms or in villages had grown up in them and looked at the world through rural eyes. The second-largest occupational group, factory workers, did not outnumber farmers for some decades after the

1870s. Until well past 1920, the American people were largely agrarian, either in actual residence and occupation or in their outlook.

As for the distribution of wealth and income, they were by no means equal in 1870 or 1880, even for the white, native-born majority. And they never had been. Yet in a nation of farmers, mechanics, shopkeepers, preachers, physicians, and the like, disparities between rich and poor were seldom great. A few nabobs could be found on Wall Street or its equivalents, and the social distance between factory owners and factory workers was palpable. But when the Civil War began in 1861, there were not yet enough factory owners or even managers to constitute much of a separate class of the wealthy. The great planters of the South were, until then, almost a feudal aristocracy, powerful enough to shanghai their humbler neighbors into supporting secession. But they were laid low by the war. Through the 1870s the South and the West-Midwest, and even the small-town Northeast, could cling to the myth and even, to some extent, the reality of an equitable, though not always equal, economic society.

Through the closing years of the nineteenth century and through the Progressive era, this preponderance of population in rural and small-town places, about two-thirds of it in the South and Midwest—regions that, except for Chicago, did not include really large cities—persisted. Yet much was changing. Immigrants from Europe entered by the hundreds of thousands in the 1880s and the millions after 1905, most of them not from northwestern Europe but from Italy, Poland, Russia, and the Balkans. Coming from czarist Russia or other monarchies, could they ever learn democratic ways?—wondered many members of the native-born white majority. While small family farms, usually called homesteads, sprouted in Kansas in the 1880s and across the Great Plains after 1900, cities grew faster, raising tough problems of public health, utilities, policing, and education. Businesses and industries multiplied, often in the form of corporations, and they grew larger and larger, making the ratio of employer-capitalist to employee-laborer ever greater. A new class arose of middle managers, neither owners nor workers but bureaucrats in railroad companies and a range of businesses. While Americans were still a rural people not only by tradition but in actuality, they were gradually urbanizing and industrializing. They were also trying all the while to figure out what that meant and how to keep the downsides from dominating them.

The late 1870s brought wake-up calls. If Henry Carey's harmonious association of producers had ever existed, it was shattered by then. Ever since a financial panic in September 1873 brought down Jay Cooke & Company of Philadelphia, the nation's largest banking house, the economy had sunk into depression. The downturn, while spotty, was severe in many sectors. Conditions did not generally improve until 1879. The worst shock was a strike of railroad workers that began in Martinsville, West Virginia, and quickly spread to Pittsburgh, Chicago, and westward in the summer of 1877. It was like no previous labor conflict; it was nationwide. The Pennsylvania governor called in the state militia. A fearful public wanted no repeat of the Paris Commune uprising of 1871 when the French capital was briefly taken over by radicals. The panicked militia fired into the crowd of strikers, bystanders, supporters, and their families. Fifty were killed. Sympathy strikes erupted along railroad lines west and east. Violent confrontations spread across New York State from Buffalo to Rochester, Syracuse, and Albany. But the upheaval was soon suppressed. Besides the dead and wounded, another casualty was confidence in "the harmony of the producing classes." If it had ever really existed, it obviously no longer did. Farmers and workers now were on one side of a great social divide, owners and managers—capitalists—on the other. No longer would Americans think in terms of harmony, but of conflict: capital versus labor, "the interests" versus "the people." Serious changes had to come. But how? Neither major political party was remotely ready for even moderate changes. Reform was years away. For thinking people, however, America had turned a corner, and around that corner were some very menacing forces.

The Great Railway Strike of 1877 was not the only disturbance. In 1882 the already large oil-producing companies controlled by John D. Rockefeller were combined into the Standard Oil Trust, forming a corporation that by itself controlled, monopolistically, a vital industry. The U.S. Supreme Court in rulings at that time defined a corporation as a legal person, in the meaning of the Fourteenth Amendment. Corporations therefore had rights, as flesh-and-blood persons did, that governments could not infringe upon. Railroads, too, were assuming corporate form, and the process was under way by which some of them would "rationalize" themselves into regional monopolies. By the late 1870s, 80,000 miles of tracks were operating, mostly in the Northeast and Midwest; by 1890 the trackage had doubled to 167,000 miles including four transcontinentals and a fifth one across Canada. Big business had become a fact of American life. And the bigger corporations became, the smaller the average worker and farmer felt, far smaller in comparison to the rich and powerful than they had ever been. Would big business require control and regulation? Only a small minority were awake to that need or possibility in 1880, or to whatever shape that would take. Only a few had any idea.

The total output of the American economy and the gross national product actually increased during the 1870s. During that decade, settlers and ranchers continued to invade the Indian lands of the Great Plains, with the most famous of several confrontations occurring at the Little Big Horn River in Montana in June 1876, when an army detachment under Lt. Col. George A. Custer was wiped out by Sioux warriors led by Crazy Horse. The national depression of 1873–78 helped end Reconstruction in the South, suppressed immigration, and demolished the security and well-being of people all across the industrializing Northeast and Great Lakes. Unemployment laid low thousands of families. Plagues of grasshoppers in Minnesota and elsewhere in the upper

Midwest "ate everything but the mortgage," but state governments refused to provide any relief. Even in well-settled and civilized Massachusetts, as of 1875, almost one in four infants died before its first birthday, and nearly one in three persons before they reached twenty-one.

Much of this was categorized as natural calamity, the inevitable risks of living, about which almost nothing could be done. Medicine was primitive. The germ theory of disease and therefore the prevention of contagion was virtually unknown or disbelieved. The fast-expanding cities were hard put to build sewerage and safe water supplies to keep up with their fast-rising populations. Infrastructure—not just the physical kind, but technological and scientific knowledge adequate to, and required for, a safe urban and industrial existence—was still lacking in significant ways. Necessity mothered such inventions through the last two decades of the century, but progress was spotty and slow. The Northeast and Great Lakes regions, the parts of the country in the throes of industrializing and urbanizing, were most immediately in need of change. But the agrarian majority also found itself deprived of economic self-determination. Railroads, the grain and cattle markets, and sellers of goods protected by high tariff walls called more and more of the shots, squeezing producers—farmers and urban workers—between low incomes and high costs.

Only two significant reform proposals surfaced in the late 1870s. One was enactment of civil service laws, which, if they worked, would ensure that public officials got their jobs through competence rather than party patronage—a laudable change but hardly one that got to the root of existing and growing social problems. The other proposal called for expansion of the currency through the issuing of paper money, or "greenbacks," backed by the faith and credit of the government, but by nothing more, not by gold or silver. Greenbacks had circulated successfully, though at a discount, during the Civil War and Reconstruction, and have been the chief national currency in recent times.

But the prevailing economic doctrine in the late nineteenth century was that precious metals had intrinsic value, and that paper currency had to be convertible into gold (preferably) or silver. This idea plagued economic thinking until well into the twentieth century. During the years 1876 to 1884, pressure grew in parts of the Midwest and East for the government to issue more greenbacks. A Greenback-Labor Party arose, and it elected several dozen members of Congress and some other public officials. But they were never numerous enough to achieve anything except denunciation of themselves as crackpots and radicals. Their proposals would become fully orthodox by the 1930s, and they still are; neither the United States nor any other developed country could operate today without paper currency *not* backed by gold or silver. But few believed it then.

Greenbackism faded from its flickering popularity by the mid-1880s. One reason was that most years of that decade were generally prosperous. Homesteading surged; immigration from Europe broke all records; markets ticked upward. A sense arose among many major-party politicians that public unrest about monopolies, and the unfairness of unprecedented and ostentatious personal wealth, needed to be listened to. The result was federal regulation of corporations, for the first time in a serious way: the Interstate Commerce Act of 1887 and the Sherman Anti-Trust Act of 1890. Prior to those federal laws, political pressure from farmers, small businessmen, and others propelled a number of state legislatures by the mid-1880s into enacting laws regulating railroad rates. It would commonly happen from this point through the Progressive era that states took the lead in reform measures, followed later by the federal Congress.

For reform to happen, pressure for regulation had to overcome the prevalent laissez-faire attitude that individuals and businesses should be free from interference. This was a long-standing axiom of American economic life. But so was opposition to monopolies, deeply ingrained at least since Andrew Jackson's destruction of

13

the Bank of the United States in 1832, which the Jacksonians denounced as a monster monopoly. By the 1880s the perception (an accurate one) had spread that railroads were all too often able to operate as monopolies, the only effective carriers of goods and peoples across long distances, and could charge shippers whatever the traffic would bear. "Shippers" included farmers selling their produce or livestock, shopkeepers buying goods manufactured elsewhere, manufacturers large and small—in short, everyone who needed to use the roads. They resented being forced to pay whatever the railroads told them to pay. As individuals they saw themselves helpless against the power of corporations (especially the railroads) far larger than themselves. The logical place to turn was state government, and legislatures obliged with regulatory laws.

Then in 1886 the Wabash, St. Louis, and Pacific Railway Company sued the state of Illinois. The Wabash claimed that Illinois' law regulating its operations violated the clause in the U.S. Constitution that reserves control of interstate commerce to the federal government. The U.S. Supreme Court agreed with the Wabash, annulling the Illinois law and, effectively, all other state laws regulating railroads.

Congress responded quickly, passing—with a bipartisan majority—the Interstate Commerce Act of 1887. Democratic president Grover Cleveland signed it in February 1887. The law demanded that railroad rates be "reasonable and just," forbade trusts and rebates to large shippers like Standard Oil, and required them to publish their rates and not raise them without ten days' public notice.

Three years later, control of Congress and the presidency had passed from the Democrats to the Republicans, but anti-trust and regulatory pressure from the public had only strengthened. Both parties campaigned in 1888 for a general anti-trust law regulating not just railroads but any trust or monopoly. Thus, in July 1890

Congress passed (and President Benjamin Harrison signed) the Sherman Anti-Trust Act. Problem solved, or so it seemed. But it was not to be. As Mr. Dooley, the fictional Chicago pundit created by the columnist Finley Peter Dunne, put it: "What you and I see as a brick wall...is to a corporation lawyer a triumphal arch." Cases reaching the Supreme Court in the 1890s (and later) whittled away at the Interstate Commerce and Sherman acts, and in fact nullified large parts of them. In an egregious instance, the case of *U.S. v. E. C. Knight Company* in 1895, the Court ruled that manufacturing—even when one company controlled 90 percent of the market—was not commerce, and therefore the anti-trust laws did not apply.

From the late 1890s into the early twentieth century, the monopolistic trend called the "merger movement" dominated American big business, consolidating all sorts of enterprises, railroads included. The consequence was fury on the part of many segments of the public. They had been fooled by the Interstate Commerce Act and the Sherman Act into thinking monopolies were under control; they had been thwarted by a conservative, business-minded Supreme Court; and they were getting the attention of their elected representatives.

The result was a demand for reform that gained powerful force during the 1890s until it reached a widespread sense of crisis by 1900. Until then, the prevailing consensus was hard to break—a consensus on Social Darwinism, that individuals were on their own to sink or swim. Perhaps the most prominent Social Darwinist was William Graham Sumner of Yale, who published a book in 1883 called *What Social Classes Owe to Each Other*. His bottom line: nothing.

In that genteel age, it was considered un-genteel to raise Cain with the social and economic order; most editors, pulpiteers, and politicians craved respectability. Greenbackers and angry farmers, in their view, were not respectable. So their complaints and remedies could be disregarded—for the moment.

Chapter 2
The crisis of the nineties, 1889-1901

In many respects, the 1880s were an expansive and prosperous time. In America and in Europe, the world seemed rich. Great architecture and engineering appeared, including the Brooklyn Bridge (1883) and the first steel-frame skyscraper (1885). Railroads spun across the continent, and by 1890 few places of any size in the Northeast and Midwest lacked passenger and freight service. Immigrants by the thousands disembarked in New York, Philadelphia, Baltimore, and New Orleans from the new and fast transatlantic steamships every day, some to stay in those port cities, more to head west. Ireland, England, Germany, and the Scandinavian countries continued to send many newcomers, but after 1880 Italy, Poland, Russia, and the multiethnic Austro-Hungarian Empire enriched the diversity.

On the Great Plains, land-seekers from the Dakotas to Texas pushed the settlement frontier ever westward. The one-time Indian Territory, first opened to white homesteading in 1889, would soon become Oklahoma. As for the Indians, their last organized resistance to U.S. forces and farmers disappeared during the 1880s, and they were confined to reservations where they were supposed to assimilate to white ways. This was the "nadir period" for American Indians—not only in numbers (from millions before Columbus to around 250,000 in 1900) but in the suppression of their cultures. Montana, Idaho, Washington,

Wyoming, and the two Dakotas—nearly the entire northwest quarter of the continental United States—were admitted as states in 1889/1890. In each, population soared, as it always had in the first years of settlement frontiers. The invasion of would-be young farmers and their families into the Great Plains did not level off until after 1915, only then ending the settlement frontier that began in colonial times.

As for the national population, the Census of 1890 revealed that in the preceding ten years it exploded by just over 25 percent, to 63 million, double what it had been just thirty years earlier, on the eve of the Civil War. The high rate of immigration, the rapid settlement of the West, and urbanization all contributed. Both urban and rural population were rising rapidly at the same time. During the 1880s, more than 500,000 new farms appeared, while the number of urban places rose by 44 percent and urban population by 8,000,000, twice as fast as rural. In every economic respect, the United States was taking its place alongside the major industrial nations of Europe, even threatening to out-produce them. Not surprisingly, it was also matching them in the social problems that headlong economic development brought with it.

The few reforms attempted during the 1880s did not go nearly far enough in meeting the new economic and social challenges that followed the Civil War. Civil service reform had been urged since the 1860s or before. In 1883, after the jolt of President James A. Garfield's assassination two years earlier, the first federal Civil Service Act, also known as the Pendleton Act, became law. It was a good start, effective in some agencies such as the post office, but it hardly ended political appointments. Regulation of big business, another obvious need, began with the Interstate Commerce Act of 1887 and the Sherman Anti-Trust Act of 1890, but they were little more than Band-Aids applied to spurting lacerations. The archconservative, pro-corporation U.S. Supreme Court soon neutered these laws. Currency expansion would have helped farmers and small manufacturers especially in the cash-poor

South and West, and it was the raison d'être of the Greenback Party. But its paper-money theory ran directly contrary to the prevailing gold-standard orthodoxy. Its advocates were tarred as rustic cranks, even though some respectable economists agreed with them. When a measure of prosperity spurred the economy after 1880, the appeal of greenbackism evaporated.

Outside of government, certain reformers promoted their programs well. Henry George advocated a "single tax" on unearned rises in real estate values, and Edward Bellamy proposed nationalizing large parts of the economy. Although Bellamy and George clubs popped up in cities across the country to promote their ideas, they chiefly attracted only educated and professional elites. The need for reforms was not yet percolating down to a broader community.

The truth, nevertheless, was that the fruits of unchecked capitalism were benefiting only a small minority at the top. Wall Street moguls and railroad barons hired fashionable architects to erect great mansions from Newport, Rhode Island, to New York City to San Francisco and, although there were never that many of them, they inspired awe, fame—and resentment. The gulf between them and the housing of the average farmer or artisan testified to the growing inequality. The United States had had its urban (and rural) poor for a long time, but the growth of large cities in the 1880s and the unprecedented immigration from Europe in that decade made poverty much more visible. Settlement houses— privately staffed institutions whose residents were the forerunners of professional social workers—began to appear as neighborhood havens to provide social services and some education to the urban poor. Hull-House in Chicago, founded in 1889, was the best-known early example, and many more followed. They could, however, reach only a small number. Poverty and inequality needed broader responses. The major labor organization of the time, the Knights of Labor, whose motto and philosophy was "the union of the producing classes," gained many successes in the early and mid-1880s, particularly against railroads, and attracted around 700,000 members by 1887. But the anarchist-led Haymarket Riot in October 1886 in Chicago tarnished the Knights even though they were not involved, because the conservative press (and public) reflexively identified "labor agitation" with anarchism. The Knights lost a major strike action in 1887, and its membership plummeted to around 100,000 by 1890. While it lasted, however, the Knights of Labor had managed to give reality to the producerite dream of an alliance between farmers and industrial workers, in the South and in some western states. By so doing the organization contributed ideology and numerical strength to the formation of the broadest and most significant reformist political movement of the post–Civil War era, the People's Party. Also called Populism, it became the strongest third party of the time.

Massive discontent began stirring in the South and the West in the late 1880s. With economies heavily concentrated in basic products (cotton in the South, wheat and corn in the West), dependent on railroads to bring those products to markets, and without much in the way of their own capital or banking systems, they were debtor regions. Southern small farmers were worse off than western ones, since the South was still rebuilding from the devastation of the Civil War. The former slaves or their children had never received the land that Reconstruction had seemed to promise, and they were thereby condemned to sharecropping or tenant farming. In the recently settled Great Plains, from Texas north to the Dakotas, a farmer and his family could fairly easily gain nominal title to land, but to work it they would usually need to borrow. The farther west they pushed, the more distant their market and the higher their shipping costs, and the more they needed money and credit for seed, fencing, tools, and more, and thus the more onerous their mortgage. The small farmers and their families of the South and the West needed easier credit and lower railroad rates. Above all, they needed more currency in circulation. That would make money cheaper and the crops and livestock they were producing higher priced, and thus bring in more cash to pay those heavy mortgages and high freight rates.

Such economic tightness had been chronic in both the South and the Great Plains since the 1870s. In the late 1880s, however, events conspired to make life tougher. In bad crop years, income was low because there was less to sell. In good years, markets were flooded and prices went down from oversupply. For the small farmers, the system was stacked against them. Politics were no help. The Union Labor ticket ran in a number of states in 1888 but remained only on the fringe; the major parties and their presidential candidates, the Democrat Grover Cleveland and the Republican Benjamin Harrison, had nothing to offer the farmers and workers. What to do? Workers could strike or boycott; farmers could not. But they could create cooperatives to protect the prices they received, and they could analyze the problems they confronted. Naturally, then, the slogan of the new, surging Farmers' Alliance became "Agitate, Educate, Organize."

By 1889 many small farmers had had enough. With support from the Knights of Labor, the George and Bellamy clubs, and ex-Greenbackers, hundreds of thousands flocked to the previously small farmers' alliances. The National Farmers' Alliance and Industrial Union, also known as the "Southern Alliance," erupted from Texas northward to Kansas, and eastward to Georgia and the Carolinas. Outraged at an economic system that enriched others, frustrated by the railroads' rates and practices over which they had no control whatever, and beset by prices so low—compared to the costs of production—that in some places it became cheaper to burn their corn in winter stoves than to sell it for almost nothing, farmers and their wives trekked to schoolhouse meetings to hear Alliance lecturers explain how the system was cheating them and what they should demand to fix it. In both regions, despite differences in how the markets for western grain and southern cotton worked, there were more than enough similarities. The Alliance program boiled down to land (easier mortgage credit), money (more currency in circulation), and transportation (equitable and lower railroad rates). To these three basic demands, others were often added, but these were the heart of the program. The Alliance movement initially stayed away from running candidates for office, but by 1890 it was clear that too few politicians in the "old parties" were listening. Thus, in some areas the Alliances began to run their own tickets. The successes were spotty but encouraging.

In June 1890, protesters and reformers of many sorts gathered in Topeka, Kansas, and created the People's Party of Kansas. Alliancemen were the core, but they were eagerly joined by Knights of Labor, single-taxers, Union Laborites, greenbackers, and Grangers. They agreed to run a full slate in November, and did so. They elected five congressmen, gained control of the lower house of the state legislature, and chose the next U.S. senator. It was a near-sweep. Kansas, moreover, was not alone. The Populists—the nickname given to People's Party voters and supporters—scored nearly as impressively in other western states and in parts of the South. The racial divide had required a separate "Colored Alliance" there, but in heavily black areas such as the North Carolina tidewater and eastern Texas, the Populists also did well—so well as to shake the control of the white-supremacist southern Democratic powers. Violent intimidation, a reprise of the Ku Klux Klan and other terrorists of the late Reconstruction era, kept southern Populists from succeeding as well at the polls as midwestern ones; though southern Populists had more raw strength than Midwestern ones, they won far fewer elections. The imminent threat of an interracial political coalition of the lower and lower-middle classes terrified the white establishment, and in the next few years state after southern state passed Jim Crow laws to exclude blacks and obstreperous poor whites alike from voting. At least, southern Populism woke up the Democratic power structure so that after 1900, in the Progressive period, the South firmly supported agrarian programs at the same time that racial segregation laws became stricter.

Populists in other states followed the Kansas lead, creating state parties and joining in the interregional movement. In 1892, more than 1,300 delegates from the South, the West, the Rocky Mountains and even a few from farther east met in Omaha to draw up a platform and nominate candidates to compete in the 1892 national election. The Omaha Platform proclaimed on July 4 was the most elaborate statement that the People's Party ever made. Its fiery preamble, written by the Minnesota reformer Ignatius Donnelly, expressed the profound indignation of millions:

> The conditions which surround us best justify our co-operation; we meet in the midst of a nation brought to the verge of moral, political, and material ruin. Corruption dominates the ballot-box, the Legislatures, the Congress, and touches even the ermine of the bench. The people are demoralized.... The newspapers are largely subsidized or muzzled.... The urban workmen are denied the right to organize for self-protection.... The fruits of the toil of millions are boldly stolen to build up colossal fortunes for a few, unprecedented in the history of mankind.... The national power to create money is appropriated to enrich bond-holders.... We seek to restore the government of the Republic to the hands of the "plain people," with which class it originated.... We believe that the power of government—in other words, of the people—should be expanded...as rapidly and as far as the good sense of an intelligent people and the teachings of experience shall justify, to the end that oppression, injustice, and poverty shall eventually cease in the land.

Because its planks inspired and often were realized by Progressives a few years later, the Omaha Platform tells us what reform ideas were already circulating that early. Some were distinctly aimed at farm problems, such as the "land, money, and transportation" issues. These had been refined and elaborated in the two or three years since the Farmers' Alliances exploded. They took the specific form of mortgage relief, regulation of railroads, and currency expansion (either greenbacks or silver coinage would do). The currency, they claimed accurately, had actually shrunk since the 1870s, squeezing the real producers, while at the same time other forms of money (such as checks, demand deposits, interbank certificates, and negotiable securities) had greatly expanded the money supply in the richer parts of the country. One Populist pointed out that a five-dollar bill that changed hands many times a day in New York or Chicago might pass only once or twice a week in their own country villages. Effectively, then, rural people had only a fraction of the currency available to city dwellers. The amount of dollars in circulation was not the whole problem; the velocity with which it flowed was crucial.

Beyond those three key issues, however, the Omaha Platform asked for other changes that would restore control of the country to "the people"—the producers—and remove it from the manipulators, the monopolists, the illegitimately powerful. It was not just a farmers' protest, but a serious critique, the first and in many ways the most comprehensive ever, of unregulated capitalism. The platform proposed deep reforms, not to abolish the capitalist system but to restore it to the people. "The railroad corporations will either own the people or the people must own the railroads," it read; hence the government, which to the Populists was (or ought to be) the same as "the people," must own the roads and run them by "rigid" civil service regulation. The platform demanded "a national currency, safe, sound, and flexible issued by the general government only"—not by national banks; "free and unlimited coinage of gold and silver" at the traditional sixteen-to-one ratio; and no less than $50 per person of currency in circulation. It demanded "a graduated income tax." It proposed "postal savings banks…for the safe deposit of the earnings of the people." Telephone and telegraph systems, as well as the railroads, "should be owned and operated by the government in the interest of the people," as was true in other industrial countries. Restriction of "undesirable" (and competitive) labor, laws requiring shorter hours for workers, and prohibition of Pinkertons and other company-hired strikebreakers led the pro-labor measures.

Populism was not, or at least so its leaders hoped, solely a farmers' movement. The Omaha Platform called also for legislation by initiative and referendum, again giving more power to "the people." It wanted voting reformed by requiring secret balloting and the Australian ballot (issued by governments, not parties, and listing the candidates of all parties, not just one). There were other demands too. But at the root of it all were two axioms: producerism, the economic theory that returns should come to the farmers and workers who produced wealth, not those who manipulated it; and democracy, the political theory that power should rest with "the people," not predatory corporations. The Populists resented the unfair control of markets, governments, and much else by those corporations (railroads, trusts, banks), and the resultant, and blatant, maldistribution of wealth.

Farmers were the majority of "the people" in the South and the West, and the Omaha Platform expressed their needs. But it also included pro-labor measures, because workers were also producers who needed help. It was a comprehensive statement of popular demands for change as of 1892. None of it would become law or policy for a good many years. In that sense, Populism failed to achieve what it advocated. But in a few years, Progressives were promoting many of these reforms. By the time they were through, much of the Omaha Platform had become state and federal law. As Worth Robert Miller, a historian of Texas Populism, accurately writes (and this fits other states too):

> The Populist appeal centered on a commitment to American republicanism....[which] mandated an opposition to monopoly and the corruption that established privilege through favoritism. Property holding was essential to individual liberty. Populists feared that the widening gap between rich and poor would drive many Americans into a dependent subservience reminiscent of European peasantry. Texas Populism encompassed those most concerned with this widening gap, namely, poor to moderate white farmers, urban laborers, and eventually African Americans.

For the rest of the 1890s, however, life for many Americans went from bad to worse. By the end of the decade a sense of crisis and impending radical change emanated from editorial pages, pulpits, and thinking people in general.

At first, the Populist surge gained momentum. A former Union brigadier general, James B. Weaver, who had been the Greenback candidate in 1880, became the People's Party's presidential candidate, with an ex-Confederate brigadier general, James Field, as his running mate. It was vital to symbolize the cross-sectional appeal, the reunion of North and South, as only twenty-seven years had passed since the end of the Civil War. Memories were still vivid. The Republican Party in the North "waved the bloody shirt" vigorously and successfully, using the memory of the Civil War as a wedge issue by repeating the sound bite, "Vote as you shot." Had there been bumpers in those days, that would have been a Republican sticker. Yet Weaver and Field won more than a million popular votes (about one out of twelve nationwide) and twenty-two electoral votes from the Great Plains westward. Theirs was the most successful third-party race up to then, and they would not be surpassed until the Progressive campaigns of Theodore Roosevelt in 1912 and Robert M. La Follette in 1924. People's Party candidates won governorships, seats in the U.S. House and Senate, and other offices. The Populists' future looked promising indeed; the inroads of 1892 might well become the highways to farmer-labor victory in 1894 and 1896.

Meanwhile, hard times worsened. The agricultural South and West were not recovering from the crop failures and low prices of the late 1880s. A major strike at the Homestead steel mill near Pittsburgh by a nascent union of steel workers broke out in late June 1892, just as the Populists were convening at Omaha. Several thousand strikers routed a force of company-hired Pinkerton agents, until the Pennsylvania governor called out the state militia and the outnumbered, outgunned strikers surrendered. The union was broken so conclusively that no large-scale steel workers' organization took form again until 1937. While farmers appeared to be winning in the West, industrial workers in the East were being crushed.

In the summer of 1893, the Reading Railroad, a major northeastern line, and another large company collapsed. Wall Street trembled, a banking panic erupted, and thousands of businesses caved in. The Panic of 1893 ushered in a depression that lasted in its severe phase until 1897. Full recovery did not come until 1901. The depression of the 1890s was the worst the United States had ever experienced, or would suffer until the Great Depression of 1929–1941. More than 18 percent of workers, by one respected estimate, became unemployed; farms folded; foreclosures and bankruptcies destroyed commerce, farms, and families across the country. Grover Cleveland, the conservative New York Democrat elected president in 1892, tried to restore confidence in the nation's finances by calling Congress into special session to repeal the government's silver purchases, authorized in 1890 to absorb western silver output and to mollify currency expansion pressure. The purchases were blamed for a frightening run on the Treasury's gold reserves. Agrarian resentment increased when Congress obliged by repealing silver purchases, and when Cleveland persuaded the banker J. P. Morgan and his associates to invest heavily in Treasury bonds—ultimately payable in gold at taxpayer expense.

The end of silver purchases ruined the economies of western mining areas. The bond sale to Morgan, the symbol of Wall Street, further convinced Populists and other agrarians that they were being victimized by corporate power. From California and the mining country, the unemployed began marching on Washington in the spring of 1894, taking over freight trains and riding across country to the dismay of public officials but the applause of many ordinary people. The marches coalesced under the leadership of Jacob Coxey, an Ohio manufacturer. Several hundred marchers in "Coxey's Army" made it to Washington. But the army of the unemployed got nowhere. The Cleveland administration had them arrested for walking on the Capitol grass, and the uprising dispersed. Yet strikes continued across the Midwest. The most famous erupted in May at the Pullman works outside of Chicago when several thousand workers walked out to protest when management cut wages by almost a third, while maintaining rents in company housing. This strike, like the one at the Homestead steel mill two years before, was suppressed abruptly by government forces—this time, federal troops sent by the Cleveland administration over the vehement protests of the governor of Illinois, John Peter Altgeld.

The conflict between workers and management, labor and capital, seriously worsened, while the condition of farmers in the South and West remained dismal. The off-year election of 1894 gave the Republicans a landslide and firm control of Congress as a rebuke to the Cleveland Democrats on whose watch the depression had begun. The Populists barely held their own. The stage was set for a climactic face-off in 1896. The economy was depressed; unemployment was unprecedentedly high; farmers were suffering. The Chicago reformer-journalist Henry Demarest Lloyd published *Wealth against Commonwealth*, a damning indictment of the monopolistic business practices of John D. Rockefeller's Standard Oil Company. Shocking and widely read, it sent the flames of reform burning higher, convincing people not so directly touched by hard times that change needed to happen.

The hope and opportunity for a new direction came with the presidential election of 1896. The Republicans nominated William McKinley of Ohio, who as a congressman became known for the "McKinley Tariff" of 1890 which "protected" American manufacturers from competition from imports. It may once have been prudent to protect America's "infant industries," but by the 1890s they were easily outselling foreign competitors. The Republican argument was that the protective tariff helped not only manufacturers but saved jobs for workers. Critics, both Democrats and Populists, denounced it for artificially and needlessly raising prices on consumer goods. It was, they complained, a tax on consumption and therefore *hurt* working families. McKinley, however, insisted that the tariff helped workers; it won them "the full dinner pail."

The Democrats came to their convention profoundly split. The eastern and conservative wing, led by President Cleveland, faced a revolt from westerners, particularly over the money standard. Cleveland stood for the gold standard, while the westerners championed the return of silver dollars at the traditional ratio of sixteen ounces of silver to one of gold. That had been the law from 1792 until 1873, when Congress quietly dropped the silver standard. Gold meant continued scarcity of money and credit; silver meant a better-lubricated flow of goods and services. Eastern businessmen, bankers, and investors were aghast at the prospect of "free silver at 16 to 1," because by then silver was overvalued at that ratio. Western and southern farmers demanded it with all their hearts, because restoring the silver standard meant reflation of the currency and a much improved ability to meet mortgage and shipping costs, indeed to survive the depression. (A century later, no less a conservative monetarist than Milton Friedman argued that if silver had never been devalued in 1873, the depressions of the 1870s and 1890s would most likely never have happened.) The western wing of the Democratic Party prevailed, nominating the thirty-six-year-old William Jennings Bryan of Nebraska. The eastern wing was horrified and would have nothing to do with him.

The Populists, bloodied from years of farm depression and loyal to the Omaha Platform, met two weeks later. Surprised at Bryan's nomination and the co-optation by the Democrats of their monetary policy, they simply nominated Bryan on their own ticket though with a different running mate, Tom Watson of Georgia. Bryan never declared himself a Populist; he was always a Democrat. He did not, however, reject the Populists' nomination.

1. William Jennings Bryan, Democratic presidential nominee in 1896, 1900, and 1908 and leader of agrarian Americans, enjoys an afternoon with his wife, **Mary Baird Bryan**, in front of their home on D Street, Lincoln, Nebraska, sometime in the 1890s.

He unquestionably represented agrarians, and he ran a vigorous campaign.

From this point until his death in 1925, Bryan was a towering figure in American politics and culture. He was also the perennial champion of the agrarian interests of the South and West—in Populist and Progressive terms, "the people." Possessed of a euphonious voice that carried far at gigantic rallies, he could thrill thousands with his message of hope and progress. Blessed with a wife both wise and intelligent, he could always count on a secure home and prudent counsel. Unfairly ridiculed for his late-in-life defense of biblical literalism at the Scopes "monkey trial" in Tennessee in 1925, Bryan was not a fundamentalist but rather a Social Gospel Christian, a seeker of a moral and better society. He reconciled biblical literalism with a thoroughgoing commitment to economic and social justice as no national leader has done since. Named Woodrow Wilson's secretary of state in 1913, the highest office he ever held, he negotiated many treaties of friendship and reciprocal trade. He resigned out of principle when he feared that Wilson was risking war by a hostile note to Germany after the sinking of the *Lusitania* in 1915. As a Democratic politician-statesman, Bryan depended on the Solid (Democratic) South, which meant turning a blind eye to Jim Crow. But otherwise, as his biographer Michael Kazin writes:

> Bryan was the first leader of a major party to argue for permanently expanding the power of the federal government to serve the welfare of ordinary Americans from the working and middle classes....He did more than any other man—between the fall of Grover Cleveland and the election of Woodrow Wilson—to transform his party from a bulwark of laissez-faire into the citadel of liberalism we identify with Franklin D. Roosevelt and his ideological descendants.

Bryan, however, lost in 1896. He won almost a million votes more than any Democrat ever had, and about as many as the combined Cleveland-Weaver votes of 1892. But McKinley won hundreds of thousands of new voters. The sins of Cleveland and the grinding depression persuaded a host of them to throw out the incumbent Democrats, even though the Democrats who were to blame, if any were, had already been supplanted by Bryan and his comrades. Almost four out of five eligible voters cast ballots, a rate that has never been equaled since. Bryan wrote a book, which he called *The First Battle*, about the campaign. That was accurate. He and the forces of political agrarianism would be back. His defeat in 1896 ended the People's Party as a force in national elections. But it did not end agrarian interests in American politics, nor efforts to forge coalitions of agrarians and industrial workers.

But such developments would have some time to wait. A degree of recovery brightened the economy in 1897 and 1898, sparked by a trend, led by investment bankers, railroad barons, and other big-business leaders, to combine and consolidate. This was not good

30

news for workers and their families, but it improved the overall economic picture. As the anti-trust and interstate commerce statutes were defanged by the U.S. Supreme Court, the "merger movement" proceeded apace until the first years of the new century. Railroads were "rationalized," as Wall Street phrased it, so as to prevent competition on routes and rates. The steel industry (or much of it) came together in the country's first billion-dollar corporation, U.S. Steel, thanks to J. P. Morgan engineering the purchase of Andrew Carnegie's holdings. Trusts proliferated in oil, rubber, copper, and a whole range of industries. Factory workers and miners—in general, wage workers who were employees of corporations—got little benefit from the reorganizations. Farmers, however, saw crop prices begin to move upward, and homesteaders once more crept westward across the high Plains after being stalled since the late 1880s.

Thus farmers and workers, natural allies in many ways against the common corporate opposition, had no obvious reason to join forces. Broad-based reform remained some time away. Reform-minded mayors had already begun to surface in a few cities, notably "Golden Rule" Jones in Toledo and Tom Johnson in Cleveland, anti-corruptionists who ran and spoke in evangelical terms often redolent of the Populists' rhetoric. More often, and almost invariably in the largest cities, the sale of streetcar franchises, the appointment of cronies to public jobs, and the buying of politicians by businessmen were the order of the day. Reform of city government, to say nothing of state and federal, would require a much more vigilant press and much more vigorous candidates than were around in 1900. In another five to eight years, all that would come—muckraking journalism, reform-ready national and state leaders, a trade-union movement that began to win some victories, both in strikes and in state laws limiting how long women could work each day, keeping children off factory floors, and more.

Patriotic causes usually divert attention from economic problems and serve as wedge issues to divide political-economic allies. So it happened in 1898. The deeply embedded American penchant for imperial ventures, somewhat quiescent for a couple of decades, was aroused by what was portrayed by pro-Cuban propagandists and elements of the American press as the struggle to free Cuba from the yoke of Spanish despotism. In Congress and around the country, Democrats and Populists rallied to the idea of helping the Cuban insurrectionists. Republicans, less sympathetic, nonetheless were stirred toward war by the explosion that destroyed the American battleship USS *Maine* in Havana harbor in February 1898—an event blamed on the Spanish, but which many years later was proved to have been caused on board. McKinley engineered a congressional authorization to send troops and ships to aid the Cubans, and in April 1898 the United States declared war on Spain.

The struggle lasted only a few weeks. American squadrons wiped out Spanish fleets in both Cuba and in Spain's other major colony, the Philippine Islands, in the western Pacific. They, with the smaller colonies of Guam and Puerto Rico, became American. On land the Americans had a harder time of it, and in the Philippines, in fact, war broke out not between the Americans and the Spanish, who departed quickly, but with the Filipinos, whom the United States were supposedly freeing. Before it was over in 1902, the Philippine "insurrection" killed over 4,200 American troops and tens of thousands of Filipinos.

In Cuba the most celebrated outcome was a cavalry charge led by the young Theodore Roosevelt, who had put together a ragtag regiment he called the "Rough Riders." Waving his sword up Kettle Hill near Santiago (not San Juan hill, as a journalist wrote), he kept on riding, figuratively, into the governorship of New York in the fall 1898 election, and into the vice-presidential nomination of the Republican Party in 1900.

Meanwhile, a peace treaty extracted by the United States at Paris in late 1898 transferred sovereignty over Guam, Puerto Rico, and the Philippines from Spain to the United States. Cuba became nominally independent, but its finances and foreign affairs would be controlled by the United States for decades. When the treaty came before the Senate in 1899, Republicans generally supported the annexation of the Philippines, with Democrats and the few remaining Populists opposed. Anti-imperialists—a varied group ranging from Mark Twain to Andrew Carnegie and leading Social-Gospel churchmen—raised serious questions, especially whether a republic like the United States could rule a colony like the Philippines and withhold the Bill of Rights from the Filipino people. But the imperialists ratified the treaty by one vote.

Other than the transfers of territory, Theodore Roosevelt's ascent was probably the most consequential outcome of this brief war. He became one of the great symbols of martial prowess and American imperialism, along with Admiral George Dewey, who won the naval victory in the Philippines. But Dewey had no political charisma. Roosevelt did. Ironically, the appearance of this militarist-imperialist on the national political scene marked the beginning, in important ways, of the Progressive movement.

By 1900 the economy was recovering, the imperial surge was subsiding, and the exhilaration and expectancy of a new century invigorated many. But not everyone. In that year, in the religious and thoughtful press—from pulpits, in editorials—a sense of deep social crisis kept being voiced. Speakers in many Protestant pulpits, and politicians of both parties, shared this sense. The spectacularly successful little war with Spain restored national pride and identity, snuffing out much of what remained of the North-South animosities lingering since the Civil War. But even the absorption of Puerto Rico, Hawaii (annexed in July 1898 during the war), and the Philippines, and control over Cuba could not disguise the country's economic and social malaise. While the depression of the 1890s was over, corporations were merging and "rationalizing," state and federal regulation was toothless, and the rich were piling up wealth. One after another state in the South passed Jim Crow laws segregating the races and preventing black people and poorer whites (the Populist kind) from voting. The McKinley administration and the Republican-controlled Congress raised the tariff in 1897 and legalized gold as the sole monetary standard in 1900, two measures that solidified corporate control of the economy and pleased the propertied classes.

But industrial workers and western farmers got little more than crumbs from the corporate table. The thrust of the Omaha Platform, that corporate greed and a supine government were dividing the American people into two classes, tramps and millionaires, appeared more well-founded than ever. Nor would the division be bridged very soon. By 1915 the distance between the richest and the poorest, or even the rich and the middle class, was wider than it would be until the Reagan era. The majority of Americans in 1900 were upset by frequent workers' strikes and boycotts but, as often as not, they sided with management and "law and order." A conservative judiciary, from district judges to the Supreme Court, backed them up. The Populists' demands for change were ignored as the economy seemed to improve, and many in the urban Northeast had always dismissed the Populists as crackpots anyway. Still, a feeling began to spread that much was wrong with the country despite the improving economy and the imperial triumphs. Economists and sociologists were thinking along new lines, undermining old certainties. Reform was in the offing. How it would take shape, and where, and who would lead it, was anyone's guess in 1900. But in a very few years Progressivism coalesced and clarified.

Chapter 3
Progressivism takes shape, 1901-1908

The presidential election of 1900 re-matched the 1896 opponents, Republican William McKinley and Democrat William Jennings Bryan. This time McKinley did a little better and Bryan a little worse. One reason was that Bryan did not have the People's Party nomination that he had in 1896. More important, McKinley profited from the rebounding economy and the exhilaration many voters felt after the victory in the Spanish war. The Republicans also gained seats in both the Senate and the House of Representatives, all-in-all solidifying the majority that they had enjoyed since 1894. Conservatism— meaning encouragement rather than regulation of railroads, manufacturers, and other corporations—was more firmly at the nation's controls than ever.

How long McKinley-style conservatism would have continued can never be known, because Leon Czolgosz, a Michigan-born self-taught anarchist, shot the president on September 6, 1901, at the Pan-American Exposition in Buffalo. McKinley lingered a few days, then died. Vice President Theodore Roosevelt, not yet forty-three, younger and more physically and mentally vigorous than any president had ever been, brought to the White House a new political era for the new century. In his nearly eight years as president, TR captivated the majority of Americans with his near-manic vigor, moralism, involvement with a host of issues, and employment of the White House as his "bully pulpit"—that is, a terrific perch from which to preach. A friend called him a fascinating combination "of St. Vitus and St. Paul." Roosevelt was a believer to the core in the superiority of the "Anglo-Saxon race," as were many white Americans then, including well-educated reformers. But he also inspired and led many reforms. By the end of his eight years in office, Progressivism had taken shape as a multifaceted movement. He was not the only reason why that was so; the growing army of settlement-house workers, crusading journalists and pastors, academics and trade unionists—many of them women—all helped weave the many early strands of reform that would coalesce later into mature Progressivism. But it all needed a weaver-in-chief. Bryan was playing that role for his agrarian followers. But Theodore Roosevelt, a Northeastern city man, thrust into the presidency, did so for a hitherto skeptical and leaderless urban constituency. It is difficult to see how Progressivism could have matured without TR to convert the skeptics, harass conservatives, and lead the weaving.

A list of the achievements of Roosevelt's first administration, from September 1901 to March 1905, is surprisingly brief. In his first annual message to Congress in December 1901 (the address nowadays known as the "State of the Union" speech, which was transmitted to Congress but not actually read by a president until Woodrow Wilson began doing so in 1913), TR called for a "Square Deal." It would consist of new laws (not many) and stricter enforcement of existing ones regarding trusts and monopolies, outlawing the rebates that railroads had been kicking back to their favorite customers such as Standard Oil, and a recognition that labor organizations might just possibly be owed some justice instead of being consistently suppressed by state or federal troops or by the courts. His Department of Justice began prosecuting trusts; it would ultimately rack up forty-four anti-trust suits. Congress took its time, but by 1903 it did pass the Elkins Act, prohibiting rebates.

Congress also, on Roosevelt's urging, created a new Department of Commerce and Labor, for the first time giving equal weight to the two. Within it was a Bureau of Corporations, which began producing authoritative reports on corporate activities, some of which provided evidence on which the Justice Department could proceed with its anti-trust prosecutions. The Bureau of Corporations was broadened in 1915 into the Federal Trade Commission, which continues to exist.

Beyond these laws and initiatives, however, Roosevelt exercised decisive executive leadership. Capping what has been called "the merger movement," several of the country's leading railroad and financial titans—James J. Hill of the Northern Pacific, E. H. Harriman of the Union Pacific, J. P. Morgan, and John D. Rockefeller—created a huge trust that they called the Northern Securities Company to bring together under one management the Burlington, the Northern Pacific, the Great Northern, and other roads. It would have created an almost complete monopoly of rail transportation in the northwestern quarter of the country. The public outcry was loud. Roosevelt, in office only five months, instructed Attorney General Philander C. Knox to bring suit under the Sherman Anti-trust Act of 1890 to dissolve the trust. Up to that point the Sherman Act had been emasculated by the Supreme Court, but in 1904, by a five-to-four decision, the court actually ruled for the government and against Northern Securities—and thus for the people.

Roosevelt made clear that in his view not all corporations, not even all trusts, were bad; there were some "good trusts." In that first message to Congress in December 1901, Roosevelt he explained the difference, writing that

> The captains of industry who have driven the railway systems across this continent, who have built up our commerce, who have developed our manufactures, have on the whole done great good to our people.... The mechanism of modern business is so delicate

that extreme care must be taken not to interfere with it in a spirit of rashness or ignorance.... Yet it is also true that there are real and grave evils... and a resolute and practical effort must be made to correct these evils.

To the fictional Mr. Dooley, Roosevelt seemed to be saying that the trusts were "heejous monsthers... created by enlightened enterprise" that should be "crushed underfoot... but on the other hand, not so fast." Regulate interstate corporations, inspect and publicize how they operate, TR urged—and the result was the watchdog Bureau of Corporations (1903) and carefully aimed anti-trust prosecutions. The caution did not please many incipient Progressives, just as the prosecutions upset many businessmen. But it was clear that the unquestioning business-could-do-no-wrong stance of Cleveland and McKinley was a thing of the past.

Even more attention-getting and public-pleasing was Roosevelt's intervention in late 1902 to end a six-month-long strike of anthracite coal miners in Pennsylvania. Represented by the United Mine Workers, the miners asked for recognition as a union, an eight-hour day, and a 10-to-20-percent pay raise. The head of the union, John Mitchell, behaved in a conciliatory, agreeable way, quite in contrast to the stereotypical wild-eyed radical striker caricatured by conservatives and management. In contrast, railroad president George F. Baer, spokesman for the mine owners, claimed that "the laboring man will be protected and cared for—not by the labor agitators, but by the Christian men of property to whom God has given control of the property rights of the country." He later announced that "These men don't suffer. Why, hell, half of them don't even speak English."

Inevitably the public-relations victory went to Mitchell and against Baer and his fellow capitalists—and to Theodore Roosevelt for appointing an even-handed (and successful) commission that solved the strike just before the onset of what threatened to be a very cold winter. Again, the president steered carefully around any implication of radicalism. He did not support union recognition, and the UMW did not get it. But he had intervened in a major capital-labor dispute in a balanced way most unlike his predecessors' almost knee-jerk dispatching of troops. He had, he proclaimed, backed the middle class, the honest workers, the producers, against the monopolists. Thus he tapped into one of the deepest-held beliefs of the American public—fairness—that went even deeper than laissez-faire individualism.

Roosevelt has been credited with great things, but in his first term the concrete achievements were limited to the anti-trust prosecutions (most notably against the Northern Securities Company), creation of the Bureau of Corporations, and his intervention in the anthracite strike. Where is the disconnect between achievements (few) and reputation (large)? It lies in the contrast between TR's attitude toward monopolies, toward labor organizations, and toward government activism, and that of his Gilded-Age predecessors. The young president, still only forty-six when his first term ended, presented the American public with a fresh face as well as a major turning away from the unflinching pro–big-business, anti-labor policies of the past. The change was not simply in measures, but, very decidedly, in tone. He had already compiled an impressive and varied resumé before 1901—he had run a ranch in Dakota Territory, written several works of history, patrolled the streets of New York as its police commissioner, led a regiment in combat in Cuba, and more. Enjoying the support of his wife Edith, his closest confidante, and the antics of their several young children, TR bestowed an exuberant spirit on a previously dour White House, rather like the Camelot of the Kennedys sixty years later. His predecessor from 1889 to 1893, Benjamin Harrison, was said to have had "a personality like a dripping cave." TR and Edith, and their entourage, were completely different—exuberant, exciting, surprising.

2. Theodore Roosevelt and Edith Carow Roosevelt sit for a family portrait on the lawn of their home at Oyster Bay, Long Island, in 1903. Roosevelt's daughter Alice (later Longworth) by his first marriage is standing in the back.

In his frustrated later years, TR sometimes grew petulant and irritable, but while in the White House he was a true hero to many. Compared with Bryan, "the boy orator of the Platte," Roosevelt's upper-class New York and Harvard upbringing was much less frightening to middle-class city-dwellers. Compared with later Progressive and liberal administrations, his achievements appear light, even overhyped. Yet in the context of the Gilded Age past and the free ride that big business had enjoyed since the Civil War, TR was fresh air, and his actions, though few, gave heart to millions.

They replied by awarding him a full term as president in the election of 1904. He won 60 percent of the two-party popular vote, and he would enjoy a nearly two-to-one Republican majority in the House of Representatives and a very safe Senate as well. Now elected "in his own right," TR felt able to take an increasingly visible position as a reform leader, much less constrained by conservative party moguls and by the need to raise campaign funds. Adroitly threatening the Old Guard of his party that he would champion downward tariff revision, which would have undercut many of the capitalist special interests that they represented, TR secured several measures that would not have been remotely achievable in the 1890s.

Immediately after the election, beginning with his annual message to Congress in December 1904 and continuing for the next four years, he moved gradually and more openly to the left. Reform sentiment of many kinds was gathering strength, and the president was both leader and follower of the trend. He recommended that Congress strengthen the Interstate Commerce Commission to the point where it could set railroad rates—to conservatives, a reprehensible infringement of property rights but to shippers (including farmers and small business people) another plain restoration of fairness. Labor unions, he said, have "been among the most effective agents in working for good citizenship." But, cautiously, he warned that they must avoid "violence, brutality, or corruption," and he refused to accept the idea of the closed shop requiring all workers in a unit to be members. Again he asked Congress to pass an employer's liability law for the District of Columbia, and for safety's sake, a limit of eight hours per shift for workers on interstate railroads. In 1906 he supported a Naturalization Act, which federalized the naturalization process and established nationwide procedures conducted by the new Immigration and Naturalization Service—a move to supervise, though not to thwart, the hundreds of thousands of newcomers arriving every year.

Responding to strong entreaties from social-justice and sanitary reformers like Florence Kelley of the National Consumers' League and leaders of the National Women's Trade Union League and the National Child Labor Committee, Roosevelt called for more information on child labor conditions and on meatpacking practices. He wanted the Interstate Commerce Commission to have the power to lower a railroad rate upon a shipper's complaint. He favored immigration "of the right kind"—industrious, thrifty—and he did not ask for literacy tests or other pet projects of restrictionists.

As in past and future years, TR called for a vigorous foreign policy, further naval buildup, and continuing work on the Panama Canal. His most famous utterance on foreign affairs was part of his December 1904 message to Congress—the famous "Police Power Corollary" to the Monroe Doctrine:

> Chronic wrongdoing, or an impotence which results in a general loosening of the ties of civilized society, may in America, as elsewhere, ultimately require intervention by some civilized nation, and in the Western Hemisphere the adherence of the United States to the Monroe Doctrine may force the United States, however reluctantly, in flagrant cases of such wrongdoing or impotence, to the exercise of an international police power.

In other words, the United States would decide on its own who, where, and when "chronic wrongdoing" was taking place, and it arrogated to itself a license to restore order. The "corollary" would be renounced in the early 1930s, but in the meantime it justified several extensive interventions in Caribbean republics, making them "protectorates" of the United States. He would "walk softly and carry a big stick," he proclaimed, and by accepting labor unions and corporations alike (if they were well behaved), the president expressed and appealed to middle-class values. In doing so, he enjoyed the lavish support of much of the public.

A year later, TR again sent Congress his annual message. Congress had done little about some of his earlier recommendations. Once more he asked for railroad-rate regulation, a final end to rebates, and employer liability for injuries to workers in the District of Columbia and in navy yards, where federal (rather than state) jurisdiction was unarguable. "The corporation has come to stay, just as the trade union has come to stay," he proclaimed. The 1905 message also included notice that the Department of Commerce and Labor would investigate not only child labor practices but the condition of women workers—a matter brought before him by settlement-house workers representing women in the packing houses and other industries who were having great difficulty unionizing. He also called again for downward adjustment of tariffs. At about this time (1908), the U.S. Supreme Court decided in favor of an Oregon law limiting the number of hours that women could work. This case, *Muller v. Oregon*, was untypically progressive for the Court in those days, but it was persuaded by the empirical evidence gathered by Josephine Goldmark of the National Consumers' League and argued by Louis D. Brandeis, the lawyer for Oregon. Glimmerings of legal and legislative support for the rights and needs of women workers were beginning to appear.

In 1906 the Republican Congress, dreading tariff reform, was aware that TR's popularity could enough generate public pressure to force passage of almost anything he endorsed. He was creating the modern presidency, backed by the media of the day. Congress finally gave him his employer liability act to protect workers in the District of Columbia and on common carriers (chiefly the railroads) in interstate commerce. The most important new law affected railroads. Soon known as the Hepburn Act (after the Ohio congressman who drafted it), it empowered the Interstate Commerce Commission to lower a railroad rate on complaint of a shipper, and it strengthened the commission in other ways. It passed in May 1906 after a bitter fight with Congress, including TR's threats to champion tariff reform, which finally broke the obduracy of Nelson Aldrich (R-RI and chair of the Senate Finance

Committee) and other "railroad senators." Roosevelt also appealed over the heads of Congress to the public to put pressure on their representatives. The law still did not satisfy some reformers, including Senator Robert M. La Follette of Wisconsin. But it was reform nonetheless.

Two more landmark measures became law a month later. These had been urged by women's clubs, health advocates, and the strong contingents of moralists in the growing reform cohorts, because they so clearly pitted decent treatment of the consuming public against corporate greed. These were a federal meat inspection law, and then a "Pure Food and Drug Act." The first aimed to (literally) clean up meatpacking, and the second restricted the sale of patent medicines, many of them laced with opiates and alcohol. Roosevelt had been pushing meat inspection for some time, and his efforts were sped along when the reformer Upton Sinclair published a novel, *The Jungle*, exposing filthy conditions in the stockyards. Again public pressure converged with the president's concern. Strong pressure came from Florence Kelley and the National Consumers' League, pushing these consumer protection laws. The National Women's Trade Union League, vigorous in Chicago, New York, Boston, and elsewhere, fought to abolish child labor, institute pensions for mothers, establish compulsory education, and improve conditions and wages for women working in factories. Although it would be years before women gained the vote nationally, and they needed it to fully achieve their reform agenda, they were a force acting through their own organizations and in cooperation with settlement-house leaders, social scientists, clerics, and others.

Progress had been achieved in 1906, though it still did not quite add up to Progressivism. TR asked for, but did not get, legislation protecting child and women workers. Republicans maintained their command of both houses of Congress in the 1906 election, and the Old Guard conservatives still controlled the leadership. In a few states and congressional districts, however, reform candidates unseated conservatives. The first signs of political Progressivism were appearing. Nonetheless, as a recent Roosevelt biographer put it, "as he moved left politically, [he] found he was alienated from his own wealthy class...he decided that federal inheritance and income taxes were needed....America would be better off if large fortunes were put to public use."

Over the next two years, Roosevelt and the Old Guard continued to grow apart, especially over his relentless fighting for conservation measures. He had backed the 1902 Newlands Reclamation Act, named after the Nevada Democrat who introduced it, which became the charter for irrigated farming and public works in the West. Over time, it greatly increased potential farm acreage and, ultimately, hydroelectric power and recreational sites. Historians have called the Newlands Act the most important piece of federal legislation ever passed for the West, rivaled only by the Homestead Act of 1862. The "big dams" of the 1930s and 1940s—Hoover, Shasta, Grand Coulee, Fort Peck, and dozens more—had their basis in the Newlands Act.

Between 1902 and 1909, when he left the presidency, Roosevelt did much more for conservation. He added 17,000,000 acres to the national forest reserves, which (like the Reagan-era Sagebrush Rebellion seventy years later) infuriated Western developers who wanted to appropriate the public domain and its resources for their own benefit. By executive order and proclamation he created dozens of new national parks, wildlife refuges, and national monuments. He consolidated administration of the forests and related resources into the Forest Service within the Department of Agriculture and named his friend Gifford Pinchot as Chief Forester in 1905. Roosevelt's sponsoring of a National Conservation Congress in 1908 again pleased reformers, the nascent conservation movement, and the middle-class public, while discomfiting the Old Guard. Conservation became a hallmark of Roosevelt's administration, and certainly with regard to the West it had more far-reaching and permanent consequences than his trust-busting. His commitment to environmentalism, based on his youthful experiences in the Dakota Territory, remained deep and consistent.

In 1907 a sharp financial panic struck Wall Street, threatening the collapse of the nation's banking system. Roosevelt was forced, through the Treasury Department, to permit the J. P. Morgan interests (which included U.S. Steel) to take over the Tennessee Coal & Iron Company, a regional competitor, at a knock-down price, in return for stabilizing the major Wall Street banks. The panic quickly subsided, but an angry Roosevelt decried "malefactors of great wealth" in a speech in Provincetown, Massachusetts, on August 20, 1907. The phrase became one of his most often quoted, but it did not save him from embarrassment later, after he left office, when the Department of Justice sued U.S. Steel for the takeover under the anti-trust laws.

By 1908 the president had moved well to the left of where he had stood in his first term or even in 1905. In the Congress he had to deal with two of the most effective conservative Republicans of the era, Speaker Joseph G. Cannon of Illinois and Senator Nelson Aldrich. Together they placed brakes on Roosevelt's moves toward Progressive reform, although it is an indicator of how far toward reform the country had already moved when, in 1909, both Aldrich and Cannon grudgingly supported a bill amending the Constitution to permit creation of a federal income tax—not with any enthusiasm, but to forestall its immediate passage. In fact, they hoped that a constitutional amendment would ultimately fail to be ratified by enough states. (It was, however, by 1913.) Aldrich, ten years earlier, had denounced the idea as "communistic." Cannon opposed TR's naval buildup, his many conservation initiatives, any talk of lowering tariffs, railroad regulation, and just about any Roosevelt action that expanded federal activity, especially executive activity, in the direction of regulation. Aldrich also opposed further railroad regulation and virtually all measures he considered "anti-business."

3. Sen. Nelson W. Aldrich (R-RI), chair of the Senate Finance Committee and of the National Monetary Commission: the face of the Old Guard. Portrait made about 1905.

Aldrich was not totally obstructionist, though Cannon was. Aldrich smoothed the troubled progress of the pure food and drug bill through Congress in 1906, and in 1908 he sponsored the Aldrich-Vreeland Act that created a National Monetary Commission to devise ways to prevent future calamities like the severe Panic of 1907. The report that Aldrich and his commission produced was decidedly pro–Wall Street, but elements of it found their way into the Federal Reserve Act in 1913.

Roosevelt's second term was marked by increasing conflict—though not stalemate in every case—between an increasingly Progressive, activist Republican president and a consistently standpat, Old Guard Republican leadership in Congress. Roosevelt biographer Kathleen Dalton has written, "Though he would be sidetracked in his second term by international crises and, on a few occasions, by his own blunders, he rarely lost sight of his boldest goal as president—using the federal government to solve the human problems created by the industrial age." In so doing, Roosevelt became a Progressive himself and helped define just what Progressivism was (and was not).

His final annual message to Congress, sent on December 8, 1908, began by reassuring the lawmakers (and other "sound government" people) that "the financial standing of the Nation at the present time is excellent." That said, he launched into a long argument for further regulation of corporations. The Sherman Anti-Trust Act could be aimed too bluntly at any "combination," said Roosevelt. Instead, what was needed was oversight of all of them, especially railroads, by the Interstate Commerce Commission. Shareholders, shippers (farmers and small businessmen), and employees all had legitimate interests, and none should get "undue and improper consideration." Telephone and telegraph companies should also "be put under the jurisdiction of the Interstate Commerce Commission." Here Roosevelt previewed a position on trusts and monopolies that he would refine and make more explicit in the next four years, when he formulated his "New Nationalism" program of comprehensive reform. He was not yet there in 1908, but the idea of continuing oversight by a federal regulator, rather than ad hoc prosecutions by the Department of Justice, was already visible.

In this December 1908 message TR asserted vigorously that the Constitution granted "absolutely and plenarily" the oversight of interstate commerce to the federal government. This "does not represent centralization. It represents merely the acknowledgment of the patent fact that centralization has already come in business. If this irresponsible outside business power is to be controlled in the interest of the general public it can only be controlled in one way—by giving adequate power of control to the one sovereignty capable of exercising such power—the National Government." Here he spoke in the authentic Progressive way. Private enterprises capable of exerting economic power over masses of people, *irresponsibly*—i.e., without responsibility to the people they controlled—had to be regulated by the representatives of those people. His sharpest words followed: "There are many sincere men who now believe in unrestricted individualism in business, just as there were formerly many sincere men who believed in slavery." This closed most of the distance from the bedrock beliefs of the Populists of a decade earlier and half a country away, and his own earlier conservatism: that the government is the people and that the government, elected and responsible to the people, must oversee the massive combinations against which individual citizens were powerless.

Roosevelt next called for legislation supportive of small farmers, small businessmen, and small stockholders. He asked for postal savings banks to "make it easy for the poorest to keep their savings in absolute safety," since large commercial banks considered small accounts too much trouble. He supported good roads—"national highways [that will] serve all people with equal justice." Finally, "There must be prohibition of child labor, diminution of woman labor, shortening of hours of all mechanical labor." A better employer liability act was essential—one had passed earlier but "slovenly" phraseology had permitted the courts to throw it out—as the United States lagged well behind European industrial nations in protecting workers in this way. And he renewed his calls for an eight-hour day for federal workers.

Some of Roosevelt's language reflected his earlier conservatism. "Class consciousness"—overeager worker protests—was "certain ultimately to fail" or "to do far-reaching damage." Society encompassed multiple legitimate interests: labor, capital, consumers—and their desirable harmony would not be helped by attacks on the courts. Yet things had changed: "What would have been an infringement upon liberty half a century ago may be the necessary safeguard of liberty today. What would have been an injury to property then may be necessary to the enjoyment of property now."

Corporations, labor relations, and the courts consumed about half of Roosevelt's lengthy message. He devoted the remainder chiefly to conservation matters—protection of "the soil, the rivers, and the forests" of the country, the need to protect (and expand) national parks and forests—and to foreign relations. The message could not remotely have been given by McKinley at the close of the 1890s, nor by Roosevelt himself in his first couple of years. He had changed, and so had the issues, the informed thinking, and the popular support. His philosophy would continue to develop, as would be evident in the "New Nationalism" that he unveiled in his speech at Osawatomie, Kansas, in 1910, and in his 1912 presidential campaign. But he had come a very long way. And so had the American people.

Roosevelt refused to run in 1908 for another presidential term. He considered himself as having had virtually two since September 1901, and two terms had been the limit since George Washington. Instead he sought a successful and proven administrator who would carry out his reform agenda. He therefore picked William Howard Taft, regarded as a success as governor of the Philippines and secretary of war. Taft defeated William Jennings Bryan, nominated for the third and last time by the Democrats. And once more the Republicans controlled the Congress, by more than forty seats in the House and nearly thirty in the Senate. A good many of those Republicans, however, especially in the

House, were no longer all hyperindividualistic, anti-regulatory, laissez-faire conservatives. Progressives had begun to win Republican primaries in safe seats. Taft's Congress would not be as dependably right-wing as those Roosevelt had had to contend with. Ironically, as the House moved left, Taft's presidency slid to the right. The impetus for progressive reform in Washington, for four years beginning in 1909, would come from Capitol Hill and not the White House.

Taft's credentials and his performance as an imperial and military administrator had endeared him to Roosevelt, largely because much of TR's own activity as president had been in those realms. Foreign affairs, military strengthening, and empire-building were no certain litmus tests of Progressivism—some Progressives were activists (TR, later Woodrow Wilson) and some were much more restrained (Bryan, for example) or frankly pacifist (Jane Addams and others). The better, though imperfect, indicator of activism or restraint was party affiliation. Since the days of Lincoln and his secretary of state, William H. Seward, the Republican Party had assumed the activist role in both domestic and foreign affairs. Activism was certainly evident in the 1890s when McKinley and the congressional Republicans annexed Hawaii (Democrat Grover Cleveland had refused to do so in 1893) and when they declared war on Spain and then annexed the Philippines. McKinley, Roosevelt, their cabinet officers Elihu Root and Taft, and senators such as TR's friend Henry Cabot Lodge (R-MA), as well as Albert Beveridge (R-IN), were energetic empire-builders. Gilded-Age Democrats were by no means shrinking violets about expansion and empire but, on the questions of Philippine or Cuban annexation in 1899–1900, they were the reluctant party and often remained so through the Progressive era. There were many exceptions both ways. But the general tendency was clear: Republicans imperialist, Democrats anti.

Given the long-term consequences and specific forms of American empire-building that came out of the Roosevelt presidency, it is well to take a brief look at it and at the presuppositions about race, Anglo-Saxon superiority, gender, and nationalism that underlay it. The American imperial activity of the early twentieth century assumed that Anglo-Saxons, which certainly included Americans, were racially superior. It also expressed a conscious virility or manliness, a form of ideological chest-thumping. These were Rooseveltian attitudes, shared by many.

Roosevelt ranks high on anyone's list of imperialist presidents. Although he did not add significantly to the United States' territorial possessions except for the Panama Canal Zone, he consolidated the territorial acquisitions from the Spanish-American-Cuban-Filipino War—Guam and the Philippines in the western Pacific, Puerto Rico in the Caribbean.

Roosevelt also oversaw the beginnings of a new variant on American imperialism: the creation of "protectorates" over small republics in the Caribbean, beginning with Cuba and eventually including Panama and the Dominican Republic (and under his successors Taft and Wilson, Nicaragua, Haiti, and Honduras). The congressional resolution authorizing McKinley to send U.S. forces to Cuba in 1898 included a paragraph, the "Teller Amendment," which denied any American intention of annexing Cuba. But by another congressional action in 1901, the "Platt Amendment," the United States claimed for itself oversight of Cuba's foreign affairs, finances, and public order. When Cuba ratified its constitution as an independent country in 1903, American occupiers made sure that the language of the Platt Amendment was incorporated into it. Thus Cuba remained under the "protection" of the United States.

Platt-style "protection" would soon extend to the other republics. There was no need to annex them; U.S. power would be exerted through civil administrators, or the U.S. Marines where "necessary." The Caribbean was recognized by European powers as an area of American "paramount interest." Roosevelt's "police power" corollary of 1904 made the rationale explicit; as he said, "chronic wrongdoing or impotence" justified American intervention. American property interests in Cuba and the other republics were thereby protected—investments in railroads, sugar and fruit plantations, and real estate. Liberty for the locals was secondary to American hegemony.

Roosevelt also oversaw, indeed orchestrated, the building of the Panama Canal. Ever since the 1840s and the days of the Mexican-American War, empire-minded Americans had dreamt of a canal between the Atlantic and the Pacific, but the financing, the engineering, and the diplomacy had proved too difficult. In 1903, however, Roosevelt saw an opportunity. Aiding and abetting a movement among Panamanians to break away from Colombia, Roosevelt sent the U.S. Navy to make sure that the Panamanian rebels succeeded, and then granted to the United States a ten-mile-wide zone within which the canal would be built. The canal opened in 1914 and was a cornerstone of American commercial and naval strategy through much of the twentieth century, as central as the Suez Canal was to Britain's Empire prior to India's independence in 1947.

TR and his secretaries of war, Elihu Root and William Howard Taft, created a general staff for the army and also founded the Army War College. With the support of Congress they added battleships and other vessels to the navy, and in 1907 Roosevelt sent the new navy, the "Great White Fleet," around the world to underscore the United States' status as a "great power." Roosevelt participated in peace conferences to end a blood-soaked war between Russia and Japan in 1905 and to settle a European crisis over Morocco in 1906. Through Taft and Root he negotiated agreements permitting Japan to expand its control in Korea and influence in Manchuria, in return for recognizing American colonization of the Philippines. There, Roosevelt watched with concern and then satisfaction at the civilian-led administration of the islands by Taft and others, and he looked forward, he told

Congress, to the day when the Filipinos were ready for self-government. But that day was in the indefinite future.

He had no more qualms about treating the Filipinos as colonial subjects than he did about controlling Caribbean republics. To him, Anglo-Saxon superiority was ratified by custom and sanctified by the best science of the day. "Scientific racism," as it has since been called, has long been discarded as not at all scientific—just plain racist—yet it seemed to justify colonialism abroad as well as Jim Crow at home. Roosevelt also accepted racial distinctions among immigrant groups. Establishing a commission headed by Senator William P. Dillingham (R-VT) in 1907, Roosevelt shared its view that "old immigrants" from Britain, Ireland, Germany, and Scandinavia were much better suited to American-style democracy than the "new immigrants" from southern and eastern Europe who by then were the majority of newcomers. Some sort of restriction was needed, the Dillingham Commission concluded. Literacy testing—excluding those who could not read or write in any language—was its preferred device. Roosevelt agreed.

With regard to African Americans, his record is mixed. He made (or attempted) some appointments of blacks to judgeships, worked to end black peonage in the South, and hosted Booker T. Washington for a lunch at the White House (which earned him hysterical condemnation from the South). But he also cashiered and punished without adequate consideration of the evidence a black army detachment falsely accused of running wild and shooting up Brownsville, Texas, in 1906. Many years later all of them were exonerated; it was Roosevelt who was, judicially, trigger-happy. All in all, though he was never the thoroughgoing segregationist that his successor Woodrow Wilson would prove to be, he partook of the Anglo-Saxonist racism that is one of the least attractive aspects of Progressivism.

Another was its moralistic intrusions into people's behavior—prohibition of alcohol, regulating sexual morality, censorship, restrictive marriage and divorce laws, and eugenics including forced sterilization of the "feeble-minded." And without doubt he was a leader of American imperialism. Progressivism, whether Roosevelt's kind or others', often contained a wide streak of moral authoritarianism.

Theodore Roosevelt's presidency, and the sharp turn that it took from his immediate predecessors', has persuaded many historians to date the Progressive era from September 1901, when he succeeded McKinley. That is easy to do and not entirely wrong. TR's presidency was critical. Difficult as it is to sympathize with his racism and Anglo-Saxonism, or his militaristic imperialism, he nevertheless inspired the coalescence of many struggling strands of reform. He was the agent of synergy and, by the time he left office, even resolute conservatives had to give way to change.

In truth, however, many reforms took place quite independently of TR's influence, and some preceded him. The private sector, and notably women even though they lacked the vote except in a few western states, surged with reform activity since at least 1889, when Jane Addams and Ellen Gates Starr founded Hull-House in Chicago. Their domain and their success was social-justice Progressivism. The 1890s, depressed and strike-ridden though those years were, produced outbreaks of reform, not limited to the People's Party and its comprehensive Omaha Platform of 1892. As early as the 1880s, many middle-class women in cities around the country organized into women's clubs and urged "municipal housekeeping" on city fathers, demanding cleaner streets, purer water, better sanitation, and sewerage systems. Ellen Swallow Richards, the first female graduate of the Massachusetts Institute of Technology, pioneered the chlorination of water from the late 1880s on. Mary McDowell not only operated the University of Chicago Settlement House in Chicago's stockyards district but also fought for the cleaning up of garbage dumps and the slaughterhouses. She was a bulwark of the women workers in meatpacking houses when they went on strike against the managers who slashed their wages. She more than anyone helped those women unionize and empower themselves. Another woman, Kate Gordon in New Orleans, spearheaded the approval of a bond issue in 1899 to pay for pure water and sewerage for that city. Using what one historian has called "the three-pronged progressive method of investigation, education, and persuasion," activist-reformist women made many cities and neighborhoods cleaner, more tolerable, and attractive. The changes they began in the 1880s and 1890s broadened in scope and geography after 1900. Contagious diseases retreated as their causes became known and publicized. As boards of health and departments of sanitation became increasingly staffed by scientifically trained people, these professionals, male and female, persuaded the public of the truth of the germ theory, despite initial resistance from physicians.

Educational improvement, in both content and accessibility, was a major focus of Progressives. In 1900 about half of the nation's children aged five to nineteen were in school; by 1920, about two-thirds. The number of high school graduates doubled during the 1890s from 44,000 to 95,000, and tripled to 311,000 in 1920. Illiteracy dropped by half, from over 13 percent of the population ten years old and up in 1890 to 6 percent in 1920. Kindergartens, which were rare before 1900, proliferated early in the century, and nearly half a million were in existence by 1920. At the other end of the educational ladder, colleges, universities, and professional schools expanded in size and in what their curricula included, as the demand for a better-educated and trained public rose as American society became more urbanized and, at least in certain sectors, more technological. "A&M" schools like Kansas State or the University of California's Davis campus traced back to the Morrill Land-Grant College Act of 1862, but after 1900 they were teaching "scientific agriculture" to promote conservation as well as profit. Medical education, previously chaotic, underwent general reform after 1910, when Abraham Flexner produced a landmark report calling for systematic licensing and standards. Legal training was changing; the traditional practice of "reading law" as

4. "True friends of the underprivileged." Jane Addams (*left*), co-founder of Hull-House, and Mary McDowell (*right*), head resident of the University of Chicago Settlement, 1914; they were among the nation's pioneering settlement house leaders.

an apprentice to an established attorney began shifting to formal study at a law school.

Change was not always rapid. But it came; and probably nowhere more innovatively than in graduate education. The first true research university, Johns Hopkins, was founded in 1876, followed by the University of Chicago in 1890 and Stanford in 1891, while established institutions such as Harvard, Yale, Michigan, Wisconsin, and the University of California at Berkeley retooled to include graduate divisions and PhD programs. As a result, professionalized social sciences (sociology, political economy, history, economics, statistics) began emerging in the 1880s and the 1890s. They provided a cadre of experts after 1900 who were essential to reforms and regulative agencies at all levels of government and in the private sector.

The new social science departments of the research universities were generally modeled on German practice, and many of the leading professors in those departments were German-trained. Richard T. Ely, who earned a doctorate from Heidelberg, was one of them, first at Johns Hopkins and then at the University of Wisconsin. He mentored many leaders in the next generation of economists, notably John R. Commons, the leading analyst of labor economics in his day. Among the new social scientists were the sociologist Lester Frank Ward, the educational psychologist G. Stanley Hall, and the historian Charles A. Beard. They had several approaches in common, all of them subversive of the rationalistic, rigid laissez-faire dogmas so commonly held and so resistant to change. They were, in the first place, historicist: economies and policies should and did change over time. They looked at society not simply as collections of isolated individuals but as organisms; people, economies, social groups did not live in isolation. Therefore policies should be based on empirical evidence, evaluated and sifted by experts in sociology, political economy, and allied sciences, who would then devise programs and policies that governments would effectuate for the benefit of the social organism. Evidence was crucial, and they collected it avidly. State and local governments instituted many agencies along these lines. Examples at the federal level were the Bureau of Corporations (1903), the Dillingham Immigration Commission (1907), and the Children's Bureau (1912), which Progressive women prodded President Taft to support. All told, they constructed a basis for political and social change that was intellectually respectable, though the agencies could become bureaucratic and dogmatic. They typified the Progressive spirit, however; and from the mid-1880s on, in increasing numbers and strength, academic social scientists provided ideas and programs for social and governmental reform.

One reason why some of the new social scientists succeeded in promoting radical social changes—and some (like Ely) aroused the wrath of conservative boards of trustees who nearly fired them—was that they couched their ideas and findings in religious terms. "Socialism" was then, as now, a word abhorrent in American parlance. Although a few such as the Episcopal priest William D. P. Bliss embraced the title of "Christian Socialist," most academics preferred to be seen not as socialists but as social scientists—although Christian ones. In this they were part of a developing movement in many Protestant denominations called the Social Gospel. A sense that unregulated, monopoly-tending capitalism was not only socially harmful but also unjust and anti-Christian began welling up in the 1880s and 1890s, especially among Protestant pastors with pulpits in larger cities who worked daily amid slum conditions and the urban poor. Some began transforming their congregations into "institutional churches," actively providing soup kitchens, recreational facilities, and safe havens for their neighborhoods. Surfacing across the range of mainline Protestant denominations from Episcopal to Baptist, the Social Gospel's common theme was that much of urban and industrial life was sinfully wrong and needed to be changed. Christianity, properly understood, demanded it. Sin was no longer only individual but social. Drunkenness and prostitution were not the only moral transgressions. So were inhumane working conditions, poverty, maldistributed wealth, and other ills.

The best theologian of the Social Gospel leadership was Walter Rauschenbusch, a Baptist pastor who worked with the poor in New York City's Hell's Kitchen, a midtown West Side neighborhood. In his book *Christianity and the Social Crisis* (1908), he condemned inadequate wage levels and economic inequality, the corporate control of city governments, and modern business as "a gladiatorial game in which there is no mercy." Summing up, he wrote,

> To repent of our collective social sins, to have faith in the possibility and reality of a divine life in humanity, to submit the will to the purposes of the kingdom of God, to permit the divine inspiration to emancipate and clarify the moral insight—this is the most intimate duty of the religious man who would help to build the coming Messianic era of mankind.

In other words, Christian people should bend their efforts to bring about the Kingdom of God on earth. It would be a mistake "to postpone social regeneration to a future era to be inaugurated by the return of Christ." Don't wait for the millennium to come around; take action now.

The Social Gospel according to Rauschenbusch and other articulate theologian-pastors spread widely among the major Protestant denominations. When the Federal (later, National) Council of Churches was founded in 1910, its ethos was the Social Gospel—and hence Progressive. The Social Gospel was so popular that it gave to Progressivism itself a Protestant tincture, and did much to legitimize reform among Protestants, particularly upper-middle-class ones. Jews and Catholics in the United States were more likely to be immigrants and/or working class, but some among them nonetheless paralleled the Social Gospelers. Examples include Chicago's Reform rabbi, Emil G. Hirsch, who preached on the need for social change and urged Julius Rosenwald, who owned Sears, Roebuck and attended Hirsch's Sinai Temple, to become a major philanthropist. John A. Ryan, a priest raised by Irish immigrant parents on a Minnesota farm, was the leading Catholic social reformer through his books, *A Living Wage* (1906), *Distributive Justice: The Right and Wrong of Our Present Distribution of Wealth* (1916), and "The Bishops' Program of Social Reconstruction" (1919), the official social-justice document of the American Catholic church. Ryan's life demonstrated the continuity of reform. As a youth he was a Populist; in middle age a Progressive; and in his later years an outspoken supporter of Franklin Roosevelt's New Deal.

Not all Protestants were Social Gospelers, however. In 1910, the same year as the Federal Council of Churches was founded, the traditionalist manifesto known as *The Fundamentals* appeared. It consisted of several volumes affirming the Virgin Birth, the literal resurrection of Jesus, and, more generally, the idea that sin is individual rather than social. If the Social Gospelers were a minority within the Protestant denominations, the Fundamentalists were a smaller one at first; but in subsequent decades fundamentalism, rather than the Social Gospel, eventually commanded more support and political influence. In the early twentieth century, the balance between sin-as-individual and sin-as-social wavered oddly, so that both theological threads contributed to support legislation regulating people's behavior, notably prohibition of alcohol and drugs. The Social Gospel was a force contributing to Progressivism, but so too, in a different way, was traditional, individualistic Christianity.

Paralleling the Social Gospel but basically secular were the settlement houses. Located in poorer urban neighborhoods, often largely immigrant, one of the earliest and best-known was Hull-House on Chicago's West Side, founded by Jane Addams and Ellen Gates Starr in 1889. The Henry Street Settlement in the Lower East Side of New York, founded by Lillian Wald in 1893, and Mary Julia Workman's Brownson House in Los Angeles (1901) were other important examples. Mary McDowell's University of Chicago Settlement in the stockyards district not only helped improve the living conditions of the Irish, Polish, Lithuanian, and other immigrant people there, but also assisted them in organizing union locals. Hull-House and settlements elsewhere educated immigrants in a wide range of subjects from English to book-binding, provided day care for working mothers and meeting space for unions and neighborhood organizations, published reports on housing and labor conditions, and fought for Progressive laws at the city, state, and ultimately the federal levels. Settlement houses were most often created and led by women, some of whom had broken educational barriers. Yet men, often socially conscious businessmen and professionals, also took active roles. Many enthusiastically supported suffrage for women and laws to end exploitation of female and child factory workers.

The Social Gospelers and the settlement house people gradually gained accelerating strength through the 1890s and during the Roosevelt presidency, although TR had relatively little to do with either. Nor was he especially pleased with the investigative journalism that appeared beginning in 1902. Technology such as the linotype (1884) and high-speed rotary presses made possible inexpensive, widely circulated newspapers and also magazines. Periodicals supported and published the research of Ida Tarbell into the machinations of the Standard Oil Company (in *McClure's*, 1902); of Lincoln Steffens into corrupt ties between corporations and city governments in "The Shame of the Cities," (*McClure's*, 1903–4); and David Graham Phillips' exposé of Senator Nelson Aldrich in "The Treason of the Senate" (*Cosmopolitan*, 1906), to list only the best known. The reform-exposé genre also included books. First came Lloyd's indictment of Standard Oil (1894), and then the widely read novels of Upton Sinclair, *The Jungle* (1906) on filthy and dangerous conditions in the Chicago stockyards, and of Frank Norris, *The Octopus* (1901) on the corrupt exercise of power by the Southern Pacific Railroad. Roosevelt, at one point exasperated by the waves these journalists were making, called them "muckrakers"—like the man in John Bunyan's *Pilgrim's Progress*, perpetually raking muck. The name stuck, even though TR and much of the public welcomed many of the tough-minded, tough-talking exposures.

All of these activities among the churches, the settlement houses and social work, and journalism, contributed to the rising spirit and pressure for reform. Seldom were they radical. They did not please conservatives but they invigorated the middle classes in both town and country. They showed that change could come without overthrowing the political and economic system—by reform, not revolution. Corporations could be reined in; poverty and income inequities could be addressed without falling into the abyss of socialism.

State and local governments started passing reform measures in the 1890s and broadened their efforts after 1900. Historians have often called them laboratories of reform, because the more successful state and municipal efforts became models for the federal-level laws that were to follow in the 1910s. A few examples, from among many around the country, demonstrate this.

Wisconsin was an early leader in reform, notably when Robert M. La Follette was governor. Collectively his programs were called "the Wisconsin Idea," and much of it was underpinned by the economic and sociological investigations carried out by Richard Ely, his student and successor John R. Commons, and others at the state university in Madison. La Follette was elected as a Republican three times to the U.S. House of Representatives (1885–91), three times as governor of Wisconsin (1901–6), and four times as U.S. senator (1906–25). La Follette enjoyed the wise counsel and constant support of his wife, Belle, who was the first woman to earn a law degree from the University of Wisconsin and was a journalist and reformer in her own right. Together the La Follettes devised, advocated, and implemented laws and policies to improve the condition of workers and farmers, African Americans and immigrants; they promoted woman suffrage; and as pacifists they opposed America's entry into World War I. Pugnacious and articulate, "Fighting Bob" La Follette began his political career as a common-garden Republican, but broke with the Old Guard in the 1890s, becoming a true reformer as governor. Decades later the U.S. Senate honored him as one of the five outstanding members in its history.

In the 1890s La Follette campaigned against corporate influence in his party, for stronger regulation of railroads, and for greater control of government by "the people." The Wisconsin Idea, the hallmark of his years as governor, included a long list of reforms: commissions to regulate railroads, civil service, the tax system, forestry, and transportation; the direct primary rather than party conventions to nominate candidates for office; more centralized public schools in country districts; and an end to corporations'

5. Sen. Robert M. La Follette (*standing*), is with his wife, Belle Case La Follette, their children, Bob Jr., Phil, and Mary, and Dr. Philip Fox La Follette, at Maple Bluff farm near Madison, WI, in 1909.

contributions to political campaigns. By no means did all of this become law. But passed or not, these reforms became standard rallying cries, aided in no small part by La Follette's tireless public speaking and advocacy. He championed woman suffrage and the direct election of U.S. senators by popular vote rather than by state legislatures (though ironically he was the last to be elected that way in Wisconsin, in 1905), two measures that later became Progressive amendments to the U.S. Constitution. After he went to Washington as a senator, his followers passed the first workmen's compensation law by an American state. The Wisconsin Idea became a model for reformers in other states— both its specific measures and its reliance on academic experts and fact-finders to place proposals on a firm factual basis.

In Kansas, another state that led in Progressive reform, Governor Edward W. Hoch in 1905 supported a primary election bill specifically modeled on Wisconsin's, including direct election of candidates for the Senate. Hoch backed further civil service reform, juvenile courts, a pure food law, and many other measures reflecting a more pro-active state government. Kansas also passed a comprehensive child labor law in 1905. Like La Follette, Hoch was a Republican, but of the growing Progressive or insurgent wing, favoring (like Roosevelt) downward tariff revision and tougher enforcement of anti-trust laws. Some of the leaders of Kansas Republican insurgency had been staunch opponents of the Populists during the 1890s, among them Salina editor Joseph Bristow, who became a U.S. senator in 1909, and Emporia's famous editor, William Allen White. For those middle-class Kansans, reform was becoming respectable, not just gripes from cranks and hayseeds. It was possible by 1905, as it had definitely not been in 1895, for a Republican to support reform measures. The prominence of Theodore Roosevelt undoubtedly contributed to this shift, but so did the increasing resentment of corporate (especially railroad) power.

In neighboring Oklahoma, on the eve of its transition to statehood in 1907, a thirty-one-year-old teacher and newspaper writer named Kate Barnard led campaigns to organize Oklahoma City workers and the city's unemployed into a local of the American Federation of Labor. She also wrote substantial sections of the new state's first constitution of that year. In 1906 she successfully led a farmer-worker coalition that inserted clauses prohibiting child labor and requiring school attendance into the new state constitution, which she regarded as her major (though not sole) contribution. The constitution also created an elected office called Commissioner of Charities and Corrections. Barnard ran for it as a Democrat in 1907, won, and thus became the first female statewide elected official in the nation. She also backed prison reform and laws forbidding the blacklisting of workers who had gone on strike. A contemporary newspaper wrote that Barnard "is to the new State of Oklahoma what Jane Addams is to Chicago—its leading citizen."

6. Kate Barnard was the young reformer who inspired much of Oklahoma's first constitution (1907) and its early social-justice laws.

In Denver, a county judge named Benjamin B. Lindsey, also thirty-one, spearheaded the creation in 1901 of a juvenile court, separating defendants younger than sixteen from adult prosecution and imprisonment. It was not the earliest in the country—Chicago had one in 1899—but after Lindsey was appointed its judge, it became the most famous and the model for many others. Like Barnard, Lindsey fought against child labor, and he promoted juvenile courts through pamphlets, books, and lectures. In his experience, young offenders were not yet fully responsible for their actions and, moreover, they could be rehabilitated. His rationale proved persuasive, and juvenile courts spread around the country.

The South developed its own brand of progressive reform. The region had never built cities and industries on the scale of the Northeast and Midwest in the decades following the Civil War. Instead it remained heavily rural and agrarian. The rise of the People's Party in the 1890s as a coalition of poor white and poor black farmers frightened leaders of the entrenched Democratic Party across the South, and from Texas to Virginia they passed Jim Crow restrictions on voting between the late 1880s and 1905. Black men and poor whites were disfranchised. So were black women, but they cooperated wherever they could with white women to win suffrage for all women.

Successful politicians certainly represented agrarian interests— white ones—but, like Republicans in Kansas, southern Democrats had been bitter enemies of the Populists. Also like Kansas Republicans, they began to adopt some of the Populists' proposals. James K. Vardaman of Mississippi, as governor from 1904 to 1908, championed prohibition, raised taxes on railroads and other corporations, sought educational and prison reforms, and later as a senator (1913–19) joined with La Follette to stop child labor. But Vardaman was also a raucous racist and defender of lynching. So was Ben Tillman, senator from South Carolina, but a strong advocate of railroad regulation and campaign finance reform. For Jeff Davis, governor of Arkansas from 1901 to 1906, white supremacy and farmers' issues went hand in hand. Oscar B. Colquitt, governor of Texas from 1911 to 1915, on the other hand, was not an outspoken race-baiter, and approved laws enacting prison reform, limits on women and child labor, workmen's compensation, and public education. Charles B. Aycock, governor of North Carolina from 1901 to 1905, was more typical in being an outspoken Jim Crow white supremacist but also a strong backer of public education. Thus Southern Progressivism was usually laced with racism against African Americans. Although northern Progressives were hardly free from the disease, in the South it affected virtually everything political.

A number of reforms that took place in the South after 1900 were underwritten by northern philanthropists including Chicago's Julius Rosenwald, a strong moral and financial backer of schools for African Americans. Rosenwald also brought Jane Addams and a trainload of northern Progressives in 1915 to Booker T. Washington's Tuskegee Institute. Washington headed Tuskegee from 1881 to train southern blacks as teachers and in industrial arts. Southerners spent northern money for Progressive causes, as did Alabama's Edgar Gardner Murphy, who in 1901 started the Alabama Child Labor Committee and in 1903 the Southern Education Board, with the eventual support of over $50 million from the Rockefeller Foundation. The eradication of pellagra and hookworm through campaigns both clinical and educational rested on funding and staffing from the Rockefeller Sanitary Commission. The General Education Board, another Rockefeller philanthropy founded in 1902, did much to improve education, public health, and sanitary conditions.

Progressivism flourished in the West. In California, reform had many faces. Conservation was one—the protection of the state's natural beauty. That brought up the question of whether private interests or local governments should control water and hydroelectric power; Progressives trusted elected governments. Yet environmentalism did not always win. Was the objective the preservation of natural beauty, or the conservation (and deployment) of natural resources? On this conservation/preservation question, the movement divided. The preservationists' leader, John Muir, and his supporters could not prevent the damming of the Hetch Hetchy Valley in the Sierras, engineered to provide water for San Francisco. Los Angeles developers built a 200-mile aqueduct from the Owens Valley on the east side of the Sierras to bring water to Los Angeles. Without the water, both cities' growth would have been strangled. Environment-conscious Progressives objected, but urban development also had some Progressive support. Californians, clubwomen and socialist women together, successfully brought about woman suffrage in 1911. Reform had its racist side there as well; California passed a law in 1913, reinforced in 1920, to prohibit Japanese immigrants from owning land.

The most prominent California Progressive was Hiram Johnson, a Republican who was governor from 1911 to 1917 and U.S. senator from then until he died in 1945. Johnson ran in 1910 against "the octopus," the Southern Pacific Railroad. His rhetoric recalled that of the Populists and of Progressives elsewhere: the people must prevail against "the interests." In his 1911 inaugural address, Johnson insisted that "the first duty that is mine to perform is to eliminate every private interest from the government, and to make the public service of the State responsive solely to the people." Government must be efficient—a Progressive watchword—and responsive. Political parties were another target of Johnson's, and he therefore advocated reforms to weaken them: the initiative, whereby ordinary citizens could (by getting enough voters to sign a petition) place a measure on a ballot if they were not satisfied that the legislature would do so; the referendum, whereby the electorate would vote on that popular initiative; and the recall, whereby the people could vote out of office an official with whom they were dissatisfied (as Californians did to Governor Gray Davis in 2003). Johnson also called for a stronger railway commission with the power to set rates; a nonpartisan judiciary; conservation in the style of Theodore Roosevelt; an employers' liability law; and more. Much of this got done, although commentators since then have pointed out that these structural reforms went too far, weakening the political parties too gravely and destabilizing the state's government by a horde of ballot initiatives that, ironically, could be ginned up by special interests or wealthy cranks. Time has shown that Progressives underestimated the power of the hated "special interests" to turn reform measures against them. A case in point was the Jarvis-Gann initiative of 1978, known as "Prop 13," which capped property taxes so severely as to damage the state's educational system and other agencies.

Oregon was another western state where Progressive reform flourished. Portland, in particular, enjoyed a sequence of reform leaders who developed what they called "the Oregon System" between 1902 and 1908. Unlike the situation in Kansas or the South, where Progressives usually had fought Populists earlier, Progressives in Portland often had Populist roots; the two movements overlapped there. During the 1890s the Oregon Farmers' Alliance, the Knights of Labor, and the trade-union federations joined ranks. In 1902, led by William S. U'Ren, the son of immigrants from Cornwall, this coalition passed an initiative and referendum law by a decisive margin, even before California did. Two years later the same people brought about a direct primary law, and in 1908 a recall measure and a corrupt practices act. Direct election of U.S. senators followed. The thrust of the "Oregon System" was, therefore, to put power directly in the hands of the voters. In 1912 Oregon became the seventh state to extend the vote to women. Direct democracy had come far, but it was not extended much farther: a measure requiring taxes to be approved only by referendum and to abolish the governor's veto power stalled after 1908, though the Populist-Progressive coalition, and its basis in farmer-labor-small-business support, continued to produce some successes.

Progressivism takes shape, 1901–1908

7. William S. U'Ren conceived and led enactment of the "Oregon System," probably the nation's most successful synthesis of Populism and Progressivism.

Oregon System historian Robert Johnston sees its success and its support as resting on a lower middle class of small home owners, skilled workers, and mechanics who were not really very different in terms of wealth and class from small proprietors; indeed, they often moved from one group to the other in the course of their working lives. These were "average citizens" who formed the mass of the voting population. Their political philosophy owed much to the producerism of the late nineteenth century and its confidence in the harmony of the "producing classes"—which decidedly did not include the capitalists who employed and exploited thousands in their factories and who thereby amassed great fortunes.

Reform in Oregon, and all across the country, rested not only on visible and vigorous leaders like Bryan, TR, and La Follette. In fact, it would have gone nowhere unless workers, shopkeepers, agrarians, and "small" professionals like teachers, librarians, ministers, and editors gave the movement a broad followership and membership. Progressivism, in government and outside of it, whether focused on tax and income reform or social justice measures and institutions or improving personal and public morality, was coalescing into a broad national movement. Agrarian ideas from the Omaha Platform and producerism joined the programs of urban reformers. Very soon these would take shape in federal legislation including the four Progressive-era constitutional amendments (the income tax, direct election of U.S. senators, woman suffrage, and prohibition).

Rarely was the coalition that produced the Oregon System replicated elsewhere with any precision. But by 1908 the many strands of reform, both in and out of politics and law, were forming a coherent—and rapidly growing—consensus for social and political change. Laissez-faire was out, governmental power in—first at the local and state levels and before long, at the federal.

The election of 1908 did not yet reveal a coherent, fully mature Progressive movement in national politics, but Republican hegemony was shakier than it looked. By 1908 nearly half of the states—a dozen outside the South—were using primary elections to select candidates for office. In a number of congressional districts, "insurgents"—the name then given to reform-minded Republicans—had toppled standpat conservatives. In some places, conservatives simply retired in the face of reform strength in their districts. This was especially true from the upper Mississippi Valley westward. Party loyalty, especially to the dictatorial Speaker Joseph G. Cannon of Illinois, was substantially weaker among the new congressmen elected in 1908, who took office in March 1909. Together they would break the grasp of Cannon and usher in the true heyday of Progressivism. The many strands of reform comprising early Progressivism, both in and beyond politics, law, and government, the promoters of social justice and women's rights, the educational reformers and the slum cleaners, would finally coalesce into a mature political movement. The day of maturation had not quite arrived by the 1908 election, but it came very soon after that—ironically, just after Theodore Roosevelt, who had played such a critical role in providing the synergy that brought the many separate demands for change to coalesce, left office.

Chapter 4
The high tide of Progressivism, 1908–1917

By 1908 local and state governments in all sections of the country had responded in their own ways to the unrest and sense of crisis that had been building up since the depression of the 1890s. The economy in general had improved since that disaster. When the financial panic of October 1907 threatened to set off another depression, Roosevelt called on J. Pierpont Morgan to rally Wall Street's resources to stop it, and they did. The upshot was relief, mixed with apprehension, among the public. People now realized that the country's financial and monetary system needed serious reform. But it could only come either from Wall Street, unelected and responsible only to itself, or from the elected federal government. Wealth continued to flow disproportionately to the wealthiest; corporations still operated with little regulation; the Supreme Court consistently ruled against labor unions.

Struggles between labor and capital marred the early twentieth century as they had the late nineteenth. Not a year went by from the late 1880s on without at least 1,000 work stoppages; more than 8,000 occurred in 1917–18, the peak years. In New York City's Greenwich Village in March 1911, 146 workers, mostly young immigrant women, died when a fire broke out on the upper floors of the Triangle Waist Company. They could not escape because management had locked the doors, and firemen's ladders could not reach high enough to rescue them. Outrage at this atrocity further added to the drumbeat of reform. Mining, one of the most dangerous and underregulated kinds of work, also begged for regulation. More than 350 coal miners were killed in a West Virginia explosion in December 1907, and another 100 died the following November in Pennsylvania. In the West, at Trinidad, Colorado, the United Mine Workers struck for fourteen months against the Colorado Fuel & Iron Company, which ignored safety measures, cheated miners on the weight of the coal they dug, overcharged them and their families at company stores, and refused to recognize the union. The company hired a machine-gun-toting detective agency to break the strike. When both sides started shooting, the governor sent in the Colorado National Guard. But when it appeared to side with the company, more violence erupted. The worst single day was April 20, 1914, when more than a dozen women and children suffocated in a pit underneath a burning tent. This became notorious as the "Ludlow Massacre." Over the next two weeks, over fifty miners and company guards died in the fighting. In the summer of 1917, at Bisbee, Arizona, a strike against Phelps Dodge and other copper-mining companies ended when vigilantes herded 1,186 strikers and sympathizers into boxcars and dumped them miles away in the New Mexico desert without food or shelter.

Labor conflicts paralleled race conflicts. An ugly race riot erupted in August 1908 in Springfield, Illinois. Several persons were killed, black neighborhoods were torched, and thousands fled the city. In reaction, white and black Progressives led by W. E. B. DuBois, Ida B. Wells-Barnett, William English Walling, and Oswald Garrison Villard joined together and in early 1909 formed the National Association for the Advancement of Colored People. Quickly augmented by settlement-house leaders Jane Addams and Florence Kelley, philosopher John Dewey, and journalists Lincoln Steffens and Ray Stannard Baker, and others, the NAACP quickly established chapters in New York, Chicago, and other cities to promote racial harmony and prevent interracial violence—which, however, kept happening.

8. William Edward Burghardt DuBois was Harvard's first African American PhD, founder of the National Association for the Advancement of Colored People, and editor of its journal, *The Crisis*.

African Americans, of whom more than 90 percent still lived in the South, were legally prevented from voting in every southern state, lived under continuing threat of lynching and ejection from whatever property they had, and confronted the most thorough Jim Crow segregation system since the end of slavery itself. Southern politicians such as Vardaman of Mississippi and Tillman of South Carolina could qualify as Progressive on nonracial issues (taxation, schools, prison reform) while they also advocated lynching as a means of social control. In the next decade, the "Great Migration" took many southern blacks northward to Chicago, Detroit, and other cities, and westward to Los Angeles, leaving behind hardscrabble farms. Segregation confronted them in the North too, but at least they no longer had to fear the South's convict-lease system (which imprisoned them on trumped-up charges and contracted them to white farmers and businessmen for pittances), a Reconstruction-era substitute for slavery.

Despite all of this social dysfunction, political reforms kept coming. Direct-primary laws appeared in state after state following 1901, and by 1917, forty-four of the forty-eight had them. In 1912 only thirteen states had primary elections for presidential electors, but more than half did by 1916. The initiative and referendum arrived on the legislative books in twenty-two states between 1898 and 1918, along with direct election of senators, in many states prior to passage of the Seventeenth Amendment at the federal level. In Wyoming, Colorado, Idaho, and Utah in 1908, women were voting for president. Washington state in 1910, California in 1911, and Oregon in 1912 joined the woman-suffrage states in the West. Besides the state and local statutory reforms, muckraking journalists continued to uncover corrupt links between businessmen and politicians, the sale of harmful drugs to consumers, insurance frauds, and more outrages. The Social Gospel and settlement houses strengthened, and professional social work began grappling with urban poverty. Wisconsin sociologist Edward Alsworth Ross published his popular book, *Sin and Society*, in 1907, maintaining that sin was no longer just an individual matter but a social one; electing good men was not enough; society required structural reform. His colleague, economist John R. Commons, kept publishing empirical studies of labor conditions, which underpinned the reform legislation of Governor Robert M. La Follette. At the University of Chicago, philosopher-educator John Dewey founded a "laboratory school" in 1896 and thereby launched progressive education, basing learning on experience rather than theory. Dewey and Harvard's William James became the leading exponents of pragmatism, regarded as the distinctly American school of philosophy, with its emphasis on practical rather than abstract knowledge—or, as James once put it, "the cash value of ideas." Pragmatism (Dewey called it "instrumentalism") helped underpin empirical research into how society really operated, which led in turn to Progressive reform laws. Professional methods and standards flourished in the social sciences (economics, politics, sociology, anthropology), history, and in medical and legal training.

The final significant action during the Taft presidency was Congress's creation in the summer of 1912 of the U. S. Commission on Industrial Relations. Leading social workers, academic social scientists, and Social Gospelers promoted it, and they gained the backing of Samuel Gompers, the head of the American Federation of Labor, and the business-oriented National Civic Federation. Taft signed the bill and proposed a somewhat conservative slate of commissioners. Proponents managed to postpone the appointments until Democrat Woodrow Wilson took office, and he appointed a more reformist group. The chair was a tough-minded lawyer from Kansas City, Frank P. Walsh. In 1916 the commission brought out an eleven-volume report recommending widows' pensions, compulsory school attendance, juvenile courts, and much more—a catalog of Progressive social-justice proposals. Some were adopted by state governments, and some by the federal. Walsh was made co-chair of the War Labor Board by President Wilson in 1918, and he promoted workers' rights to organize, to a living wage, to an eight-hour day, and to equal pay for women. Walsh also fought for civil liberties in the face of the anti-sedition craze of 1918–20. His philosophy, a bridge between Progressivism and the New Deal of the 1930s, was well stated in an essay that he wrote for Labor Day, 1918:

> According to the theory which was...handed down to us, the
> chief function of government has been to protect property while

leaving human beings free to acquire it. In practice, as we know, the function of government under this dispensation has only too often been the protection of property owners in the exploitation of human life.... Permit me...to join with you in celebrating this Labor Day as a day of promise that the right to dividends shall never again be paramount to the right to live.

All of these were urban-based changes. They were an important and indelible part of the Progressive record. Progressivism undoubtedly gained much of its support, certainly its most articulate and visible support, from editors, professors, politicians, and professionals, and women promoters of social justice in many forms. These reformers lived in cities large and middling, in the Northeast, the Great Lakes states, and the West from Denver to the Pacific Coast. Of the "big four" national Progressive leaders, only Theodore Roosevelt qualified as a city person, born and raised in patrician circumstances in New York. The media of the day were based in larger cities, and not surprisingly, urban reform absorbed media attention. But Bryan was not urban-formed, La Follette had a small-town background, and Woodrow Wilson was a southerner.

Thus cities were by no means the only sources of Progressivism. A key element of the movement—certainly the basis of its successes at the federal level—has often been overlooked. That element was its strong agrarian base. It's crucial to keep in mind that the United States prior to 1920 continued to be a largely rural society, in which the majority of its people lived on farms or small country villages, and that much of the economy and employment was still in agriculture or related to it—the thousands of Main Streets in small towns and cities, the mail order houses and farm implement factories in larger ones, the auto and tractor industries, the railroads, and much else, as well as the great many who actually farmed. The South was the most rural region (over 77 percent in 1910), but the Midwest (especially the Great Plains states) and West continued to have rural majorities before 1920. Only the Northeast was majority-urban, which it had been since 1880.

Agrarians—not just farmers, but small-town dwellers whose economic activity related to or depended on agriculture and who lived their lives in small-town or rural cultures—had the potential to dominate political action. Their voting strength dominated many congressional districts in the South, Midwest, and West. In urban districts, working people who might have joined the agrarians were only one of many interest groups and had to compete with corporations and others for the attention of congressmen. Thus, despite the continuing efforts of Bryan and other agrarian leaders, labor and labor unions provided the agrarians with only weak and sporadic support. The great agrarian victories of 1910 to 1917 in winning progressive federal legislation came from southern, midwestern, and western Democrats, and from insurgent Republicans in the Midwest. As the political scientist Elizabeth Sanders observes, "It was periphery [agrarian] Democrats and their less numerous northern labor allies who provided the foot soldiers for the progressive program."

The People's Party of the 1890s, together with the Bryan Democrats in 1896, tried to forge an intersectional (West-South), interracial, farmer-labor coalition. But the Populists foundered on the rocks of the divisive race issue in the South, which their opponents used to race-bait white voters. When Populists assured each other that "they are in the ditch just like us," a Southern Democrat might answer, "but they're not like us; they're black." For many, race trumped class. Southerners hesitated to break away from their traditional Democratic allegiance, or Midwesterners from their GOP, for the People's Party. Also, Bryan failed—not for want of trying—to win workers' support in the cities of the Great Lakes and the Northeast.

By around 1905, however, it had dawned on many in the South and the Midwest (and West) that one did not have to be a Populist to be an agrarian. The economic interests of farmers and those connected with agriculture outweighed political labels. One could be an agrarian Democrat, like Bryan and many Southerners. One could be an agrarian Republican like La Follette, George Norris, or Gilbert Hitchcock of Nebraska, or formerly anti-Populist Kansas Republicans like Joseph Bristow, Victor Murdock, or William Allen White. Furthermore, although the Populists had been insufficiently respectable for the Bristows and Whites, their ideas made increasing sense and eventually gained support. Bryan's agenda from 1896 for the next twenty years was largely drawn from the Populists' Omaha Platform of 1892. Of that document's proposals, the agrarians never won national ownership of the railroads and the telegraph system; or the subtreasury, the pet project of the Texas Populists. They fell well short of fundamentally democratizing the capitalist system. Nevertheless, during the 1909–18 years, they succeeded in pushing an astonishing want-list through Congress and into law: lower tariffs; a federal graduated income tax; stronger anti-trust laws; more circulating currency (not silver but even better, government-backed paper); federal dollars for agricultural education, farm marketing, and highways; backing for co-ops; election of U.S. senators by popular vote instead of (corruptible) state legislatures; and, in the continuing hope of labor support, laws regulating work by women and children.

Labor support continued to be anemic, partly because the courts permitted anti-union practices like blacklisting and would not allow collective bargaining. Agrarians still tried coalition-building, and thereby handed labor some victories. According to Sanders, "Despite the common description of the Progressive reform leaders as representatives of the urban business and professional classes, the farmers were the most numerous constituents for expanded public power in the southern and midwestern states where the reform movements were strongest."

Republican insurgents contributed their voices and votes to the cause, but the agrarian agenda depended on the much more numerous Democrats, many from the post-Reconstruction "Solid South." That solidity first arose in the 1870s in opposition to Republican Reconstruction's efforts on behalf of the newly freed slaves. Hence a vicious pro-lynching racist like Mississippi's Vardaman could at the same time be a strong Progressive.

The constitution of Oklahoma, when it became a state in 1907, was inspired by Bryan, written in part by Kate Barnard, and was a model of Populist-Progressivism, perhaps the fullest statement ever of Democratic agrarian radicalism. The northern Great Plains states were home to many agrarian Democrats. Kansas was an exception, but there Republican insurgents like Bristow and Murdock were being elected. From west Texas northward through Oklahoma, Colorado, Wyoming, and Montana, the Plains were experiencing their most exuberant period of in-migration and homesteading; 1913 was the peak year in American history for "proving up"—getting final title—to homesteads. The homesteaders were not politically conservative. As Eric Rauchway has pointed out, the votes for the progressive agenda "came from Democrats in the South and West who supported Bryanism....These Americans did not have to travel to a position from which they could support corporate regulation; they were born there." Eighty percent of Progressive legislation that would be enacted from 1909 to World War I happened when agrarians were in power. In short, when "middle-class reformism diverged from working-class and agrarian desiderata, it failed." And this agrarian preponderance helps explain why prohibition of alcohol became the Eighteenth Amendment to the Constitution in 1918, and why the Jim Crow system became so entrenched in the South, with a less violent but still real version of it in northern cities. By the 1930s these measures became iconically illiberal, but before then they were part of Progressivism.

The 1908 election, as noted earlier, put William Howard Taft in the presidency and returned a Republican Congress, but changes were on the way. The first, and some say *the* most fundamental reform of the entire Progressive era, was the passage through Congress of the Sixteenth Amendment to the Constitution, permitting a graduated income tax. In the 1990s and 2000s loud voices on the right have clamored for a "flat tax"—an income tax with only one or at most two rates that would apply to everybody—on the grounds of "fairness" and "simplicity." This view is the same as that of Gilded Age conservatives who opposed the graduated income tax. That age, like the Reagan era, was a time of increasing shares of personal income going to the richest 5 percent or 1 percent of the people. The flat tax would encourage further imbalance. The graduated tax—depending on how steep its rates actually were—would halt or reverse that trend. It is worth looking closely at why and how the American Congress and people were persuaded, early in the twentieth century, to adopt the Sixteenth Amendment.

A federal income tax had been tried before. During the Civil War, the Union government imposed an income tax as part of a medley of fund-raising devices, but it ended soon after the war. The Populists' Omaha Platform of 1892 called for a graduated income tax. Early in 1894, William Jennings Bryan argued in Congress for an income tax, though only on 2 percent on incomes above $4,000, without graduation. Bryan cited six European countries that had had income taxes for decades. To Republicans' objection that the tax was "class legislation" and would fall more heavily on the Northeast, he replied, "why should not those sections pay most which enjoy most?" He quoted Adam Smith, whose *Wealth of Nations* (1776) is widely regarded as the founding document of capitalism: "The subjects of every State ought to contribute to the support of the Government, as nearly as possible in proportion to their respective abilities; that is, in proportion to the revenue which they respectively enjoy under the protection of the State." But tariffs—customs duties, which the Republican party traditionally promoted at high levels to protect its manufacturer base—were "a tax upon consumption" that "the poor man by means of it pays far out of proportion to the income which he enjoys." Presenting figures from the *Political Science Quarterly* stating that 91 percent of American families owned 29 percent of the wealth and 9 percent owned 71 percent, Bryan asked, "Who is it most needs a navy?...Who demands a standing army?" Not farmers or workers, but capitalists who require protection for their huge properties. In 1894 the income tax passed the Democratic-controlled Congress as part of the Wilson-Gorman tariff act, following Bryan's argument that it was more equitable than high tariffs, and also as a practical matter to replace revenue lost from lowering tariff rates. But the Supreme Court declared in 1895, in the case of *Pollock v. Farmers' Loan & Trust* (a 5–4 decision), that the income tax was unconstitutional because it was a direct tax on property and was not apportioned according to states' population.

There the matter stood until 1908. The Democratic platform of that year called for income and inheritance taxes. Theodore Roosevelt, in his parting message to Congress in December 1908, agreed. By then resentment at the growing gap between the few rich and the many poor, and at high tariffs as a tax on poor consumers, had spread even among Republicans. Increasingly the talk was not only of the need for an income tax, especially if tariff rates were lowered, but a *graduated* income tax. As the Columbia University economist E. R. A. Seligman pointed out, a flat rate

> will...be felt with relatively more severity by the average man who has only a small surplus above socially necessary expenses, than by the average man who has a proportionately larger surplus....[I]n the United States the burdens of taxation...are becoming more unequally distributed, and the wealthier classes are bearing a gradually smaller share of the public burden. Something is needed to restore the equilibrium, and this something can scarcely take any form but that of an income tax.

There were only two ways around the Pollock decision. One was to pass the income tax as a normal law and then court-test it, in the hope that the current Supreme Court would reverse the 1895 decision. The other was to amend the Constitution. In July

1909, Congress chose the second route. Republican insurgents like Albert Cummins of Iowa and La Follette joined Democrat Champ Clark of Missouri, who admitted in Congress that "we would much prefer making an income tax part of the tariff bill rather than to vote for...submitting an income-tax constitutional amendment for ratification to the States." They realized that an amendment was risky because it would die if only twelve state legislatures rejected it. At best, it postponed the tax for as long as it took for enough states to ratify it—which turned out to be nearly four years. Nelson Aldrich and others of the Old Guard, with Taft's support, were able to avoid adding the income tax to the tariff bill and thus they forced the matter toward a constitutional amendment.

The debate in Congress unveiled few new arguments except to reaffirm Bryan's position of years before, that those who got the most from society owed the most in support of it. The amendment did not include the word "graduated," which might have killed it. The Sixteenth Amendment (as passed) does not contain the word. But several senators assumed that graduation would be a feature of any tax bill based on the amendment. As Nebraska Republican Norris Brown said, "The power to tax includes the power to grade." On July 5, 1909, the Senate approved the measure without a negative, and on July 12 the House passed it overwhelmingly. The amendment slowly acquired the necessary approvals from state legislatures. Those in the West, the region where income was most evenly distributed, voted unanimously in some cases, nearly so in others. Utah was the only exception. In the South, one-time Populist areas gave the income tax its strongest support. Surprising the pundits, the Northeast assented, except for Pennsylvania, Rhode Island, and Connecticut, where old-guard Republican party organizations still lived despite the insurgent wave. The *Hartford Courant* repeated the now-standard argument, that "the bigger a man's income, the greater the amount of protection he received from the government and the greater his obligation to sustain it."

Across the country, the income tax passed because agrarians, labor, and middle-class people became convinced that it was fair, that other taxes like the tariff were not, and that the distribution of wealth and income had become grossly unbalanced. The income tax amendment passed in time for the Revenue Act of 1913 to include a set of graduated rates. By then, the presidency and both houses of Congress were in Democratic hands.

Did the Sixteenth Amendment really fix income inequality? In part. The share of the top-earning 5 percent fell from about a third of all income in 1913–16 to about a quarter by 1919, but not more. It could hardly have done so because it affected so few people, and only at rates that seem ludicrously low today. In the 1913 law, the tax began at 1 percent of incomes over $20,000 and graduated to a maximum of 7 percent on income over $500,000. At that time, the highest-earning 1 percent received about 15 percent of all income, and the top 4 percent received 33 percent of all income. In 1918, according to one authority, "about 86 percent of persons gainfully employed had incomes of less than $2,000 per annum," with the upper 14 percent earning above that, for a total of 40 percent of all personal income. In 1918 the oil tycoon John D. Rockefeller owned 1.6 percent of the entire national wealth—$192 billion in 2010 money, more than twice as much as Bill Gates and Warren Buffett combined. Federal income from tariffs fell by a third between 1909 and 1916, while revenue from income taxes almost doubled. The federal tax system had undoubtedly been seriously revised in a democratic, fairer direction. In the discussions of that day, it is striking how often, almost universally, proponents of the income tax talked of fairness, of society, and of what its members owe to each other—terms that have been strikingly absent in talk in the 1990s and 2000s about a "flat tax."

Despite the passage of the income tax amendment, insurgent Republicans in Congress had reason to be disgruntled as 1909 wore on. The Republican platform of 1908 called for lower tariffs, and President Taft called Congress into special session for that purpose. A bill introduced in the House by New York congressman Sereno E. Payne did so, but Senator Aldrich produced a substitute that actually, on average, raised tariffs. Taft went along. Then the "Ballinger-Pinchot controversy" erupted. The insurgents, following Roosevelt's lead, strongly supported conservation of natural resources. Taft's new secretary of the interior, Richard Ballinger, made available some public domain lands for private development, reversing his conservationist predecessor. Gifford Pinchot, a patrician friend whom Roosevelt had appointed head of the U.S. Forest Service but who now had become a subordinate of Ballinger's, publicly criticized Ballinger over a personnel matter. Taft backed Ballinger and tried to conciliate Pinchot. But in January 1910 Pinchot criticized Taft in an open letter to an insurgent senator and called for Congress to investigate Ballinger, which it did that spring. Taft fired Pinchot for insubordination. Insurgents were outraged. The wedge widened between them and Taft, who appeared to be siding increasingly with Aldrich, Cannon, and the Old Guard.

At that same time, House insurgents managed to curtail the autocratic powers of Speaker Joseph G. Cannon. The Speaker's powers not only included control over all House proceedings. He also chaired the Rules Committee—nothing can come before the full House without a "rule"—and dominated other committee appointments. The insurgents, led by Nebraska congressman George Norris, and supported by the Democrats, put through a resolution removing Cannon's control of the Rules Committee, and the Speaker's iron grip was gone. Two months later the insurgents passed the Mann-Elkins Act, substantially strengthening the Interstate Commerce Act and requiring railroads to justify any rate increases. Taft and the insurgents were not far apart on Mann-Elkins, which proved to be the sole significant new law of 1910. But on every other issue, the Republican Party was badly split.

By the summer of 1910, Roosevelt was back from an extended safari to Africa that he began shortly after leaving office. Awaiting him was a disgruntled group of insurgents, as well as a new book by Herbert Croly titled *The Promise of American Life*. TR read the book and talked with Croly and with Progressive friends and supporters. He deeply regretted not having run again in 1908 and was incensed at Taft's lurch to the right, as the insurgents saw it. On August 31, at Osawatomie, Kansas, Roosevelt delivered a speech he called "The New Nationalism." Adopting some of Croly's ideas, and expanding on his own December 1908 final message to Congress, the speech went some distance toward full-blown Progressivism. Croly's critique of "the corruption of American public life," of "glaring inequalities of condition and power," of "economic monsters," of the corporations that "were able to secure and to exercise an excessive and corrupt influence on legislation," dovetailed beautifully with Roosevelt's opinions—as did Croly's explicit praise for Roosevelt and critique of Bryan. Much was wrong in American social and economic life, in Croly's and Roosevelt's view. The way to right those wrongs was redistribution of wealth through a graduated inheritance tax, stronger labor unions, and overall, a sense of "collective purpose" rather than unbridled individualism.

In his "New Nationalism" speech at Osawatomie, Roosevelt declared that "every man holds his property subject to the general right of the community to regulate its use to whatever degree the public welfare may require it." This brought him closer to true socialism than he had ever been, well beyond his farewell message. Differences have arisen "between the men who possess more than they have earned and the men who have earned more than they possess." To redress this imbalance, TR believed, was "the central condition of progress," the bringing-about of "equality of opportunity for all citizens." Therefore, "I stand for the square deal.... Not merely... for fair play under the present rules of the games, but... for having those rules changed so as to work for a more substantial equality of opportunity and of reward for equally good service." And so, "We must drive the special interests out of politics.... Every special interest is entitled to justice, but not one is entitled to a vote in Congress, to a voice on the bench, or to representation in any public office." Specifically, Roosevelt called for thorough regulation of railroads and all other interstate corporations; for graduated income and inheritance taxes; for banking reform to prevent future panics; "an efficient army and a navy large enough to secure for us abroad that respect which is the surest guaranty of peace;" conservation of the nation's resources; wage and hour laws; workmen's compensation acts both state and national; regulation of child and women's labor; and a "New Nationalism" that "puts the national need before sectional or personal advantage."

The congressional election was only two months away. Roosevelt's "New Nationalism" speech further energized Progressives within the Republican Party. Bryan and his renewed Populism had a similar effect among the Democrats. Bryanite Democrats and insurgent Republicans alike demanded further regulation of railroads, more conservation measures, graduated tax rates, postal savings banks so small depositors could have accounts (which banks were refusing to do), and more direct democracy of the Oregon type including primaries. In both parties, agrarians were prominent—southern ones among the Democrats, midwesterners among the Republicans. In the November 1910 election, the Democrats won decisive control of the House of Representatives for the first time since the election of 1892. Republicans dropped from 219 seats to 182, while Democrats rose from 172 to 230, gaining in the West, the Northeast, and most of all in the Midwest—23 in Illinois, Indiana, and Ohio. The Senate remained in nominal Republican control, 51 to 41, but the Democrats picked up 12 seats, mostly in the West and Midwest, and some of the Republicans were insurgents who soon voted with the Democrats. The new Sixty-second Congress had, in effect, Progressive majorities.

Taft was no standpat reactionary like Senator Aldrich, but the insurgents painted him as a betrayer of the Roosevelt legacy. In so doing they pushed Taft toward the right in 1911. This happened despite the fact that his Department of Justice prosecuted twice as many anti-trust suits, in half the time, than the Roosevelt administration had. Taft also signed into law a string of reform measures passed by both the Republican-majority (1909–11) and Democratic-majority (1911–13) Congresses. These included the Mann-Elkins railroad regulation act in 1910, free postal delivery for rural residents ("RFD"), postal savings banks, and in 1912, thanks to persistent pressure from the settlement-house and social-justice reformers Florence Kelley, Lillian Wald, and Julia Lathrop, the creation of a Children's Bureau to keep track of "all matters pertaining to the welfare of children and child life."

In May and June 1912, Congress passed the Seventeenth Amendment to the Constitution, providing for popular election of U.S. senators, ending election by state legislatures. It was a popular reform, part of the strong democratizing urge of Progressivism, and a victory (to use Progressive language) of "the people" over "the interests" who were suspected, as muckrakers had made clear, of having corrupted state legislatures. As one wit put it, "Standard Oil did everything to the Pennsylvania legislature except refine it." As for primary elections for president, thirteen states had some form of them by 1912. In some states the primary strengthened insurgency. But in the South it strengthened segregation by keeping blacks away from the Democratic primary, which was much more decisive than the general election.

Taft's four-year administration cannot, therefore, be regarded as backward or wholly unprogressive. In foreign affairs, it continued Roosevelt's activism in the Caribbean and east Asia. It accomplished considerably more than the average. But it is most remembered for something the president hardly wanted: a profound split between Progressives and conservatives in the Republican Party, which would lead to his defeat for re-election in 1912.

After the Republicans lost the House of Representatives in the 1910 election, insurgent Progressives within the party began to rally behind Wisconsin senator Robert M. La Follette as their presidential candidate in 1912. La Follette was the most prominent among them. He had founded his own weekly newspaper and the National Progressive Republican League to promote his candidacy and program, which featured primaries, the initiative and referendum, and popular election of senators. His object was to gain Progressive support and defeat Taft for the Republican nomination in 1912. But it quickly became clear by late 1911 that Taft was not La Follette's main problem. Theodore Roosevelt was.

Roosevelt, after much soul-searching, declared in the winter of 1912 that "my hat is in the ring." La Follette was greatly upset. In a February speech at a dinner of the Periodical Publishers' Association, he unloaded his resentments on the press so vehemently in a rambling speech that the episode was interpreted uncharitably as a nervous breakdown, and his candidacy collapsed. Roosevelt won most of the few primaries. Taft, meanwhile, had quietly outmaneuvered him and collected a majority of the delegates to the Republican convention and command of the Republican National Committee, which was to award more than 250 delegates. It gave nearly all of them to Taft. Roosevelt, having dawdled, never caught up to Taft's control of the Republican party machinery. At the convention in Chicago in June 1912, the Taft forces won the early procedural votes, including credentials fights. The remaining La Follette supporters swung behind Taft, and he was renominated. In historian Lewis L. Gould's words, the convention "was a bare-knuckle affair" wherein the reputedly genial and mild-mannered Taft had outboxed his pugnacious predecessor.

Later that month, Democrats gathered in Baltimore to nominate their presidential candidate. House Speaker Champ Clark of Missouri led the aspirants in the early balloting, but he could never quite reach the two-thirds majority that Democratic presidential nominations required at that time. Woodrow Wilson, the governor of New Jersey, slowly picked up delegates, and when Bryan—still a major power in the party and author of the platform—announced his support, Wilson went over the top on the forty-sixth ballot. He had been elected governor of New Jersey only two years earlier, his only elective office. Prior to that, he had been a political scientist professor, then president of Princeton University for eight years. Born in Staunton, Virginia, to a pro-Confederate Presbyterian minister and his wife, Wilson earned a PhD at Johns Hopkins and joined the Princeton faculty in 1890. Wilson was a brilliant scholar, a compelling speaker, but personally stiff. Someone once remarked that everybody called Roosevelt "Teddy," but nobody ever called Wilson "Woody."

Early in August 1912, TR and his supporters met in Chicago and stomped out of the Republican Party, shouting "We stand at Armageddon, and we battle for the Lord." Roosevelt became the candidate of the National Progressive Party—often called "the Bull Moose party" because TR, asked in June how he felt, proclaimed that "I feel like a bull moose." Governor Hiram Johnson of California, the West's most prominent Progressive, was nominated for vice president. Over the summer, Roosevelt became more and more upset, simply unable to accept the fact that Taft had outmaneuvered him. The Bull Moose platform reflected many of the social-welfare ideas in Roosevelt's Osawatomie speech two years earlier, but it also called for national women's suffrage and promoted minimum wage laws, still a radical idea. So was his advocacy of popular recall of judges and judicial decisions, which lost him Republican moderates. TR, with "his divided heart on race," declined to accept a racial equality plank offered by the NAACP. Many black voters thereupon supported Wilson, which they later had cause to regret. After taking office, the Virginian segregated the Post Office Department and refused to veto a law banning interracial marriage in the District of Columbia.

The two Progressives' reform programs were quite different. Roosevelt continued to call his "the New Nationalism." Wilson countered with "the New Freedom." The two agreed that change was urgently needed, that "the people" and not "the interests" should rule, that government—the federal government—had an important role to play, and that a better society meant better lives for its individual members. They did not agree on how to reach these goals.

For Roosevelt and the New Nationalism, big businesses—the corporations—were not going to go away. They had demonstrated a large capacity for selfish, undemocratic behavior. The solution was stronger federal regulation, specifically through agencies independent of Congress and the executive branch, like the Interstate Commerce Commission created in 1887 and beefed up several times since. But the commission needed even more power. In addition, the Bull Moose platform pressed for social justice and the democratization of government through laws limiting the hours that women and children could work; a minimum wage; old-age pensions; and workmen's compensation. The New Nationalism was a shopping list of many of the most-talked-about reforms, with strong federal regulatory commissions the centerpiece, to make sure they were carried out.

Wilson's New Freedom appeared less radical (or less Progressive, depending on one's viewpoint) but it was simply Progressivism of a different kind. Roosevelt was leading a breakaway movement from the Republican Party. Progressive Republicans would provide his support if he were to have any. Therefore the measures and methods he projected reflected the reform desires of the urban-industrial Northeast and upper Midwest, the areas of reform-Republican strength, measures quite familiar, in many cases, for having been tried in various forms at the state level. Wilson's job, on the other hand, was to energize what we would today call "the Democratic base," which was, chiefly, the agrarians of the South and the Midwest. The New Freedom therefore had to reflect the long-standing states-rights convictions and traditions of the South, as well as the interests of agrarians of all sections.

Certainly the Democratic Party had been introduced to plenty of reforms under Bryan's leadership, and it would continue to back them under Wilson. Progressivism, Wilson-style, emphasized breaking down economic combinations (i.e., trusts and other large corporations) by vigorous anti-trust prosecutions; severely lowering the tariff, which did not protect farm products but taxed farmers as consumers; and getting control of banking and the currency away from the Morgans and other big bankers and into the people's hands. The New Freedom reflected the more agrarian, less urban-industrial Democratic constituency, stressing a return to smaller-scale competition and equal opportunity, using government more sparingly than the New Nationalism—certainly not through regulatory commissions. Wilson, in his speeches, proclaimed that he did not want the federal government to control the economy, as Roosevelt seemed to be asking, but to use government to remove barriers to competition such as the tariff and the trusts and thus, one might say, to "level the economic playing field." Government would then get out of the way. Wilson claimed that "ours is a program of liberty and theirs [the Bull Moosers'] is a program of regulation." Unlike the New Nationalism, Wilson and the Democrats did not propose woman suffrage, which was too radical for the South. A few years later, only one southern state legislature (Tennessee's) ratified the woman-suffrage amendment.

Party platforms reflect what party activists would like to see happen. The Democratic platform of 1912 opened with a call for tariff reform, because "the high Republican tariff is the principal cause of the unequal distribution of wealth [which] makes the rich richer and the poor poorer...the American farmer and laboring man are the chief sufferers." It next demanded strict enforcement and strengthening of "the criminal as well as the civil law against trusts and trust officials." Then it reaffirmed states' rights (a nod to the South); called for laws putting into effect the new constitutional amendments for the income tax and direct election of senators; supported presidential primaries in every state; and advocated banning campaign contributions from corporations. The platform wanted "railroads, express companies, telegraph and telephone lines engaged in interstate commerce" regulated to protect (agrarian) consumers and shippers. It opposed a central bank (for fear it would be Wall Street-dominated), and called for rural credits to protect farm property, vocational (especially agricultural) education, a federal labor department, conservation of natural resources, and related measures. In foreign policy the platform demanded independence for the Philippines, echoing Bryan's anti-imperialism of 1898. In this, the Democrats parted company from the colonialist Republicans.

Besides Roosevelt and Wilson, who occupied the Progressive middle in 1912 in their different ways, the campaign had two other significant candidates: Taft on the right, and Eugene V. Debs, candidate of the Socialist party, on the left. He and American socialism (and why there was so little of it) deserve a few words. The words "socialist" and "socialism" have been used so often in the past by right-wing American politicians to mean anything that promoted the common good or social justice that they have become debased. The actual American Socialist Party in the early twentieth century stood for "one big union" of all workers, echoing the Knights of Labor and Populist motto, the "unity of the producing classes." The Party also called for common ownership of the means of production, and thus the consequent obliteration of corporations. Socialists at first divided over whether violence should be used to combat capitalist managements, but the Party remained nonviolent, splitting with its radical (and to some extent anarchistic) wing, the Industrial Workers of the World.

Socialism's great leader in the Progressive period was Eugene V. Debs. From Terre Haute, Indiana, originally a Democrat, Debs became active in labor organizing. He established the American Railway Union, which led the Pullman strike of 1894. Debs was arrested, spent six months in prison, and came out more than ever convinced that corporate capitalism had to be stopped for the good of working people. A charismatic speaker, he became the Socialist Party's presidential candidate in 1900, and again in 1904, 1908, 1912, and 1920. He waged that final campaign from jail, where the anti-sedition enforcers of the wartime Wilson Administration had sent him for twenty years. (President Warren Harding released him on Christmas Day, 1921, after Debs was confined for two and a half years.) Debs, according to a recent commentator, "invited working people of every class to fashion a society marked by personal generosity in private life, shared responsibility in the political economy, and genuine solidarity across all those boundaries that divide people and crush their spirit." He believed profoundly in economic democracy and the common good.

In the four-way election of 1912, Debs won more than 900,000 votes, about 6 percent of all those cast. It proved to be, percentagewise, the Socialist Party's best performance ever in presidential elections. Historians have often questioned why Debs and socialism did not do better, since many who heard him speak responded despite themselves to his eloquent championing of the brotherhood of man, the demands of social justice, the wrongs of corporations and governments that backed them. The early twentieth century saw socialist parties form and do well in other industrializing countries. The British Labour party, the Social Democrats in Germany, and the Socialists in France gained much more popular support and permanence than the American Socialist Party, despite Debs's extraordinary oratorical gifts.

A German economist, Werner Sombart, published a small volume in 1906 that asked in its title, "Why in the United States is there no Socialism?" His basic answer was that the standard of living of working men and their families was much higher in the United

9. Eugene V. Debs founded the American Railway Union in 1894 to fight the Pullman strike. A charismatic speaker, he was the presidential candidate of the Socialist Party five times from 1900 through 1920. This photo was taken during the 1912 campaign.

States than in Europe. "On roast beef and apple pie, all socialist utopias founder," he wrote. In America a worker could actually get ahead, escape rigid class barriers, and enjoy some of the good things in life. Many others have asked the same question and come up with other answers: The American Socialists were too overtly Marxist. (But the British Labourites were more so for a long time.) Federal and state governments repressed them. (But that happened in places where socialists became much stronger.) The American political system is structurally unfavorable to third parties. (There is something to that, but the failure of third parties has often meant the co-optation of their ideas by one of the major parties, such as the Democrats and even the Republicans taking over many of the Populists' proposals. Core Socialist proposals, on the contrary, such as common ownership of the means of production, remained unco-opted.) Sombart's "roast beef and apple pie" verdict contains much truth; workers' wages and living conditions were indeed much better in the United States than in Europe, which goes a long way to explain the high immigration of the time. Workers in the United States, so many of them immigrants, were divided by language and ethnicity, which corroded class solidarity. Some observers insist, too, that socialism did succeed in the United States despite winning only 6 percent in its best election, arguing that many ideas that originated with the Debsian Socialists eventually became law, although not until the 1930s, 1960s, or even the 2000s.

The election results in the fall of 1912 did not surprise many people, even those who lost. After Roosevelt and his Bull Moosers left the Republican Party, it was expected that Wilson and the Democrats would sail to victory. Some analysts believe they would have done so even if the Republicans had stayed together—that Roosevelt, and certainly Taft, would have lost to Wilson if either one had been the Republican nominee. As it happened, Wilson won forty states and 433 electoral votes; Roosevelt, six states and 88 electoral votes; and Taft, two states and 8 electoral votes, the least ever by a sitting president running for re-election. The Senate result was 51 Democrats, 44 Republicans, and one Progressive. The Democrats picked up 63 House seats while the Republicans lost 46. Progressives won 17, joining 291 Democrats and 127 Republicans. The Democrats thus controlled both the White House and the Congress.

In the long run, 1912 was a trend-setting election, but in a contrary way. Republican conservatives never re-admitted the Bull Moosers to their Party, and for much of the twentieth century the GOP hewed to the right, never again approaching the moderate Progressivism of Roosevelt's second term and never again nominating a presidential candidate as far left—as Progressive—as Roosevelt. A few, such as Ronald Reagan and

John McCain, have claimed that TR was their model, but the facts do not back them up; they abhorred the strong regulatory state that Roosevelt advocated. The Democrats, on the other hand, not only represented much of the agrarian majority of the country in 1912 but, through a vigorous legislative program, set the stage for the New Deal and Great Society that Franklin Roosevelt and Lyndon Johnson created later in the century.

Wilson, when he took office in March 1913, called Congress into special session. Presidents since Jefferson had merely sent their messages to be read, but Wilson broke precedent and personally appeared, New Freedom in hand, on April 13, 1913. As his platform promised, his priorities were to lower the tariff; to bring the banking and currency system within popular control; and to stiffen the anti-trust laws. Within the next two years, he and Congress succeeded in passing these three reforms, along with a number of specific measures that benefited farm people and workers.

The accomplishments of Wilson and the 1913–15 Congress have been called "the first New Freedom." There would be a second in 1915–17, more overtly loaded with social justice measures and benefits to farmers and workers. The most productive years of the Progressive movement, beginning in 1911, would end when the United States entered World War I in April 1917.

Wilson and Congress first tackled tariff rates, the number-one item in the 1912 Democratic platform. The argument was that high tariffs—which the Republicans' Payne-Aldrich tariff of 1909 had set at average rates of over 40 percent—picked the pockets of consumers because it unjustifiably raised the prices of what they had to buy. By May, Congressman Oscar Underwood of Alabama led a bill through the House of Representatives lowering the average to around 25 percent. Tied to the bill was a tax on incomes, made possible by the newly-ratified Sixteenth Amendment. The bill had rougher sailing in the Senate, but it passed in September, and Wilson signed it into law in October as the Underwood-Simmons tariff.

The income-tax provisions became law as the Revenue Act of 1913. As in the debate over the Amendment in 1909, the most telling argument in favor was that those with the greatest ability to pay, those whom society most highly rewarded, should pay the highest tax rate. In 1913 there was less hesitancy about graduated rates than in 1909. Still, the rates that were enacted were far from confiscatory. People earning under $3,000 as individuals or $4,000 as married couples were wholly exempt. Those earning $20,000 (at least ten times the average) would pay 1 percent; those earning $500,000 and up (in today's dollars, about $10 million), a tiny minority, would pay the maximum rate, 7 percent. Whether the bill would have passed, or whether the Sixteenth Amendment itself would have passed in the first place if legislators had suspected that rates would rise well into double digits before long, can never be known.

Wilson turned next to banking reform. Many people—bankers, farmers, small business owners, practically anyone who had any money or earned it—wanted reform of the anarchic system that had grown up since the Civil War. They remembered the depressions of the 1870s and 1890s and the Panic of 1907; bank failures and currency scarcity played major roles in all of them. But what kind of reform? Since the Populist days of the 1890s, agrarians had demanded more currency in circulation, but not in the control of bankers, especially the big Wall Street banks. Bankers, on the other hand, understood very well the need for mechanisms to avoid panics and runs, but believed they were best suited to oversee the banking system with a federal-government guarantee of its ultimate solvency. The banker viewpoint had emerged from the National Monetary Commission, widely known as the Aldrich Commission, created after the Panic of 1907.

After the Democrats gained control of Congress following the election of 1910, they launched an investigation into what they called the "money trust." It was the mother of all trusts, they claimed, because it controlled money itself, and therefore credit, and thereby, the economy as a whole. For two years the "money trust" investigation, headed by Louisiana congressman Arsène Pujo, took testimony from bankers and others up to and including the august J. Pierpont Morgan himself. In November 1912, Morgan testified that his bank held deposits of $100 million for seventy-three interstate corporations; that he himself was a director of some of them; and that the credit-worthiness of an applicant was up to his sole judgment. "The first thing is character," Morgan declared, not collateral. He admitted that his bank was entirely private and not subject to state or federal regulation or any public control and should not be. To Morgan, this was the natural and preferable state of things. To Pujo and much of the public, this was a blatant admission of irresponsibility.

Somehow the two positions—the bankers' and the agrarians'—had to be reconciled. Several bills tried to do that. Finally, with Wilson's personal intervention, a hybrid emerged that created up to a dozen regional banks, owned by their private member banks, but supervised by a federal reserve board appointed by the president and confirmed by the Senate. The regional reserve banks would issue currency ("federal reserve notes," as they were called then and ever since) that would be backed by the federal government. The regional reserve banks had the power to provide member banks with funds in the case of a panic or a run—in short, they could act as a "lender of the last resort," one of the classic functions of any central bank. In the 1907 Panic, that function was undertaken by Morgan and a few other bankers.

As a consequence of the Pujo hearings, the public demanded greater public accountability. The Federal Reserve's "last resort" powers were not used effectively at the onset of the Great Depression, when thousands of banks failed during the Hoover presidency (1929–33). Nevertheless, the 1913 Federal Reserve Act created the first truly national system since Andrew Jackson refused to renew the charter of the Second Bank of the United

States in 1833. "The Fed" became the United States' counterpart to the Bank of England and the central banks of other major countries. The bill passed the House in September and the Senate in December, with the Democrats virtually unanimous and the Republicans split. Wilson signed it on December 23, 1913. Of the three great projects of the First New Freedom, only a new anti-trust law remained to be written.

The Sixty-third Congress remained in session, except for short breaks, almost until the 1914 elections. In the spring of 1914 it passed the Smith-Lever Act, named after Senator Hoke Smith of Georgia and Congressman A. F. Lever of South Carolina. It tied vocational education in agriculture and home economics to the land-grant college system that had existed since 1862. It also threw the support of the federal government to farm cooperatives, leading to the system of county agents to assist farmers in conducting more efficient, scientific crop-growing and stock-raising. These efforts would be funded jointly by the federal government and the states, the first such joint-funding arrangement that within a few years was employed to establish the federal highway system. Ironically, although Smith-Lever was in every respect a pro-agrarian measure and had the support of less affluent and Democratic farmers, the county-agent system became in due course a bulwark of larger, more affluent, and more conservative larger-scale farmers. It was nonetheless a significant and typical part of the New Freedom program. Wilson signed the act on May 8, 1914.

The final major measure of the First New Freedom was anti-trust legislation. Here Wilson took something of a right turn, as the economy slipped into recession. Having accomplished the first two of his priorities (lowering the tariff and reforming the banking system), Wilson moved ahead on anti-trust legislation in the spring and summer of 1914. A measure to strengthen the 1890 Sherman Anti-Trust Act, which the courts had largely eviscerated, bore the name of Alabama congressman Henry Clayton. That bill specified many devices and practices of trusts considered reprehensible and contrary to the public interest, and it passed the House in May. But it stalled in the Senate.

At that point, Wilson's adviser, lawyer Louis D. Brandeis, came to Wilson's aid. He suggested that the president throw his support behind another bill wending its way through Congress, one that would create a powerful regulatory commission that would identify and pursue unfair business practices as they arose. It would provide more flexibility than the Clayton bill. Republican Progressives, the former Bull Moosers, favored this kind of trust regulation over the more rigid, nit-picking (as they saw it) Clayton version. A powerful regulatory commission was just what Roosevelt had promoted in 1912, while a statute like the Clayton bill had been Wilson's tactic. Nevertheless, Wilson swung behind the commission idea. The Federal Trade Commission Act passed the Senate in early September, and Wilson signed it on September 26. About two weeks later, a watered-down Clayton Act became law as well, merging the two approaches of the New Freedom and the New Nationalism.

Together the two acts succeeded in putting teeth into anti-trust regulation. The acts exempted labor unions and agricultural cooperatives, and thereby ended the courts' habitual rulings that strikes and boycotts were "in restraint of trade." Moreover, the Clayton Act affirmed that the labor of a human being was not an article of commerce. Agrarian southern and western Democrats were most solidly supportive of the pro-labor sections. Commission decisions were subject to judicial review, and the courts did not always agree with them. Yet Wilson had come through on his promise to seriously improve the anti-trust laws.

The congressional election of 1914 quickly followed. About sixty House seats shifted from the Democrats to the Republicans, but the Democrats still held a safe thirty-four-seat majority. They actually gained several Senate seats. In both houses, Wilson's

Democrats (together with Progressive-party congressmen, who generally voted with them) could continue to pass New Freedom measures. Not much of note became law in 1915, except an act on March 4 for the protection of merchant seamen, sponsored by La Follette. It outlawed their exploitation by ship owners and officers by such practices as low wages, bad food, indefinite hours, and abandonment in foreign ports with back pay owing. Ultimately, it became the most important law that La Follette contributed on the federal level.

Wilson, for his part, was preoccupied with personal matters—his first wife's death in August 1914 and his near-whirlwind romance and second marriage in late 1915. He was also becoming enmeshed in foreign affairs, sending U.S. Marines into Haiti (as he had done in Nicaragua in 1914 and would do in the Dominican Republic in 1916), siding with factions in revolutionary Mexico, and above all trying to avoid involvement in the World War that erupted in Europe in August 1914. When a German submarine torpedoed the British ocean liner *Lusitania* in May of 1915, killing 128 Americans on board, Wilson protested strongly—too strongly for the pacifistic Bryan, who resigned as secretary of state.

In 1916 and early 1917 a flurry of significant measures passed the Sixty-fourth Congress, and Wilson readily signed them into law. In July came the Federal Farm Loan Act, providing credit to small farmers through cooperatives. In August, another act created the National Park Service, pulling together the many national parks, monuments, and historic sites into one agency, pleasing conservation-minded Progressives. In the first week of September alone, the president signed four more significant laws. First came the Keating-Owen Child Labor Act, prohibiting interstate commerce in any goods made by children under fourteen years old. (The U.S. Supreme Court invalidated Keating-Owen in 1918 in the case of *Hammer v. Dagenhart*.) Two days later, Wilson signed the Adamson Act, giving railroad workers on interstate runs an eight-hour day. As a safety measure—statistics

10. President Woodrow Wilson and his second wife, Edith Bolling Galt Wilson, in a photo taken after their marriage in 1915 and before his incapacitating stroke in 1920.

showed that longer workdays sent accidents soaring—it was badly needed. On September 7 followed the first federal Workmen's Compensation Act, providing medical coverage for federal workers suffering job-related injuries. Finally, the Revenue Act of 1916 became law on September 8, raising income tax rates, taking the top rate to 15 percent, applicable to incomes of $2,000,000 and up. With American entry into World War I becoming an unwelcome though distinct possibility, the federal government needed more money, and this act helped; it also began federal inheritance taxes and "excess profits" taxes on businesses. In 1917, after the country actually went to war with Germany, Congress had to raise rates sharply higher yet. Had there been no income taxes, the United States might well have lacked the money to fight World War I.

Congress and President Wilson thus created a Progressive record on which to run in the impending election of 1916. Wilson had achieved much of what he had promised in his New Freedom platform four years earlier. Renominated, he faced only one serious challenger, the Republican Charles Evans Hughes of New York. Wilson won, but it was close. The Progressive Party once more nominated Theodore Roosevelt, but he refused to run, and no one took his place. Wilson won 49.4 percent of the popular vote, much better than his 41.9 percent in 1912. But Hughes won more than the combined TR and Taft vote of 1912. Wilson squeaked by in the electoral vote, 277 to 254, with late-reporting California inching him over the top. If all of the still-disgruntled Roosevelt voters of 1912 had gone for Hughes, Wilson would have lost. The Democrats' future was cloudy. Wilson's 1912 victory had depended on Roosevelt's defection, and his second owed much to the campaign slogan, "he kept us out of war," which events would belie very soon. The Democrats' majority in the House of Representatives fell to only six seats, and they lost three senators. The Republican Party still failed to recapture the majority it held before 1911, but it would do so in 1918. The high tide of agrarian Progressivism had passed.

The final session of the Sixty-fourth Congress produced the last New Freedom legislation. The first measure, the Immigration Act of 1917, must be included on the Progressive list, but it can hardly be called part of the New Freedom because Congress passed it in February 1917 over Wilson's veto. It required that immigrants be able to read English or some other language. Literacy test proposals like this had come before Congress as far back as 1896. Through the early years of the twentieth century it was the preferred device of Immigration restrictionists, including the Dillingham Commission, which presumed that it would cut down on the numbers coming from southern and eastern Europe while permitting the "more desirable" northern and western Europeans to enter. The literacy test never achieved that goal, so in 1921 a more frankly racist act became law, establishing quotas by nationality, the "less desirable" peoples being drastically reduced or completely shut out. The 1917 act also barred almost anyone from an Asian country. Immigration restriction was part of Progressivism, or at least part of the agenda of many right-wing Progressives.

A few more New-Freedomite laws, with agrarian support, came out of Congress. March 1917 brought the Jones-Shafroth Act that conferred citizenship on Puerto Ricans, and the Smith-Hughes Vocational Education Act, extending the Smith-Lever provisions of 1914 and supporting teacher training and other instruction in agriculture, home economics, and industrial occupations. It was the final labor- or education-oriented legislation of the Progressive era. Within a month, the United States entered World War I. Progressivism was not quite dead—the constitutional amendments for prohibition and woman suffrage were yet to come—but the agenda of 1910 to 1917, of laws promoting social welfare, more democratic governmental structures, income taxes and lower tariffs, and a central bank, had been exhausted.

Chapter 5
Calamities: World War I and the flu epidemic, 1917–1919

When he took office, Woodrow Wilson remarked that it would be ironic if his administration had to deal mainly with foreign affairs. The impressive list of New Freedom measures from 1913 to 1917 suggests that it did not. Nonetheless, Wilson was immediately plunged into foreign involvements in Mexico and the Caribbean, and his second term was consumed by American involvement in World War I.

Wilson's experience and leanings, and the issues that propelled him into the presidency, were truly in domestic rather than foreign affairs. In this he was quite unlike Theodore Roosevelt, who eagerly played the mediator's role in other countries' disputes, who (he admitted) "took Panama," and who after 1914 stridently demanded that the United States enter the war on the side of France and Britain. He even asked the president for a military command. Wilson turned him down, knowing that there could be no cannon more loose than a General Roosevelt. TR spent the war in petulant frustration. Wilson did find himself pulled into foreign affairs where, lacking extensive experience, he fell back on his often rigid idealism.

The immersion of the United States in the Caribbean began with McKinley, grew under Roosevelt and Taft, and enjoyed much more support from Republicans than Democrats. Yet

Wilson not only continued U.S. imperialism in that region but extended it. When he took office in 1913, the Panama Canal was nearly finished. Cuba and Nicaragua were nominally independent but remained "protectorates" of the United States, and Wilson kept the Marines in Nicaragua. When disorder erupted in Haiti in 1915, he sent in the Marines, and they stayed until 1934. When the Dominican Republic blew up in 1916, he sent the Marines there as well, and they remained until 1924. Puppet governments ran both countries. In January 1917 Wilson signed the purchase of the Danish West Indies, which became the U.S. Virgin Islands. From those islands on the east to the Panama Canal on the west, the Caribbean had become an American lake.

"Wilsonian idealism" means the approach to foreign matters that seeks to spread—or if necessary, impose—American virtues such as democracy, freedom, public morality, and the rule of law in other places—fine ideals, but not always suited to those places. At about the time that Wilson took office in 1913, a general named Victoriano Huerta seized power in Mexico and murdered his predecessor. Wilson refused to recognize Huerta's government and, to undermine him, sent warships off the Mexican coast. After some sailors on shore leave caused an incident, Wilson had Congress authorize him "to use force to bring Huerta to terms." Marines landed at Veracruz in April 1914 and stayed until November. Nineteen were killed, as well as at least two hundred Mexicans. Huerta departed, and Wilson recognized his "constitutionally legitimate" successor. Mexico remained in a virtual state of anarchy, however, and about a year later one of the faction leaders, Pancho Villa, raided towns along the U.S. border. Wilson responded by sending 11,000 troops under General John J. Pershing to chase Villa. They never caught him. With entry into the European war imminent, Wilson ordered Pershing and his force to return home in January 1917. Mexico finally got a stable government in 1920, but Wilson and his idealism had nothing to do with it.

Serious as the interventions in the Caribbean and Mexico were, Wilson and the United States faced the much greater problem of staying out of the European war that began in August 1914. When it broke out, Wilson called for Americans to remain neutral in thought and in actions. By April 1917, however, Americans had loaned the Allies (mainly Britain) more than $2,000,000,000, Germany only $27,000,000. Wilson resisted involvement yet found it impossible not to be drawn toward the Allied side. The *Lusitania* sinking on May 7, 1915, caused Secretary of State William Jennings Bryan to send a note of protest to the German government, calling for an end to U-boat attacks. Wilson regarded the German response as inadequate and proposed a second, stronger note. To Bryan, this note would lead straight to war, and he resigned on June 9 rather than send it.

War with the United States did not follow—yet—and Germany did suspend submarine warfare. The Wilson administration nevertheless went ahead with "preparedness," a rapid military buildup, in the event that the Germans resumed submarine attacks. If they did, the second *Lusitania* note strongly suggested that the United States would consider that to be a casus belli, and would declare war on Germany. In June 1916 Congress authorized a near-doubling of the size of the Army, and in August provided several hundred million dollars for new warships. Bryan, Senator La Follette, Jane Addams, and other Progressives opposed the preparedness effort, but many Democrats and most Republicans in Congress backed Wilson. Progressives in Congress, however, led by Nebraska's George Norris, insisted that those who would benefit from the new arms buildup—munitions makers, shipyards, and investors—should pay for it. They saw to it in September that the Revenue Act of 1916 doubled the basic income tax rate from 1 to 2 percent, raised the surtax on high incomes to a maximum of 15 percent, included a graduated inheritance tax, and put special taxes on munitions makers and corporate profits. The United States was not even in the war yet, but Progressives in both major parties were beginning to divide over how much "preparedness" to support.

Some believed they could have both preparedness and pacifism. Until early 1917, Wilson did not disappoint them. He tried to bring the Allies and the Central Powers together, and on January 22, speaking to the Senate, he called for "peace without victory"—a negotiated armistice. This fell flat with much of the public, and neither the Allies nor the Germans took it seriously. To the contrary: Germany, gambling on a quick end to the immobilized, murderous trench warfare that the western theater had become, announced on January 31 that it was resuming unrestricted submarine warfare. Wilson broke diplomatic relations on February 3. In March, as the last of the late New Freedom domestic legislation wound through Congress, German submarines sank five American merchant ships. On April 2, Wilson asked Congress to declare war on Germany. The Senate voted immediately to do so, 82 to 6, and the House followed four days later, 373 to 50. Wilson declared war that day.

The House vote showed that a minority of Progressives, but a substantial one, remained unpersuaded that America should enter this war. Jeannette Rankin of Montana, the first woman ever elected to Congress, voted against the war declaration. Progressives Jane Addams and Randolph Bourne opposed American involvement. But John Dewey, just as much a Progressive, fully supported it, as did many other reformers. The general public swung behind the president, as it almost always does in such situations. World War I—for the United States, not for the exhausted Europeans—was, to the contrary, a "good war," a fight portrayed as for democracy against tyranny; and it was quick, allowing little time for anti-war sentiment (aside from the pacifist minority) to develop. The first American troops arrived in France on June 26, and ultimately the United States would send roughly 2,000,000. Next summer and fall, the American Expeditionary Force had a decisive effect in bringing the war to its end on November 11, 1918.

Very soon after the American declaration of war, legislation from Congress and executive acts from the administration centralized the economy for the war effort, repressed anti-war dissent, and revealed a dark side of the Progressive urge. Regulation of private enterprises of all sorts, from farms to the railroads, was unprecedented and thorough under the new War Industries Board. The National War Labor Board was charged to mediate disputes and avoid strikes. The Committee on Public Information under George Creel bent public opinion in support of the war. "Liberty Loans" raised money by selling war bonds to the public. The Selective Service Act of May 18, 1917, drafted young men and quickly created a much larger army. A month later, Congress passed an Espionage Act, and in May 1918 a Sedition Act. Together they legitimized the most draconian limits on free expression since the Alien and Sedition Acts of the John Adams Administration in 1798—except that the 1917–1918 laws were far more stringently enforced. More than one thousand people were convicted under them, particularly the Socialists; under them Eugene V. Debs received his twenty-year sentence. On October 16, 1918, a new immigration act excluded "aliens who believe in or advocate the overthrow by force or violence of the Government of the United States or of all forms of law" or "who disbelieve in or are opposed to all organized government." The target was alien immigrants, but the victim was opinion, no matter how private, now considered grounds for deportation or arrest.

For more than two decades, pressure had been building among many Progressives to prohibit the sale of alcoholic beverages. Although obviously a measure that impinged on personal behavior, prohibition was not regarded at the time as foolish, futile, and invasive of privacy, as it later came to be seen, but a question of public health, safety, and morals. Since 1874, the Women's Christian Temperance Union had publicized the harmful effects of alcohol use and urged that it be banned. Beginning in 1880 the Prohibition Party ran candidates for president, and in almost every election from 1888 to 1920 its candidate won more than 200,000 votes. Dry laws passed in states and localities, covering about three-fourths of the country by 1917. Certain

Christian churches favored prohibition, as did Progressives who saw alcohol as a destroyer of families and homes and a major contributor to poverty, slums, and other social evils. In that sense Prohibition was a Progressive reform.

After the United States entered World War I, momentum built for a constitutional ban on the sale, manufacture, and importing of liquors. There were war-related reasons: beer was seen as a German product; the war effort needed the grain. Accordingly, after several tries, Congress in December 1917 passed what became the Eighteenth Amendment and sent it to the states for ratification. On January 1919 the necessary thirty-sixth state ratified. An enabling act named after Minnesota congressman Andrew Volstead passed Congress in October 1919, and nationwide prohibition began in January 1920. It lasted until the amendment was repealed in 1933.

As hundreds of thousands of American troops landed in France, President Wilson looked ahead to the shape of the peace. Speaking before Congress on January 8, 1918, he announced a fourteen-point plan. It too was an unmistakably Progressive document, Wilson-idealist variety. The first point was "Open covenants of peace, openly arrived at"—i.e., no more secret treaties. Then, "Absolute freedom of navigation upon the seas"; international trade free of "all economic barriers"; reduction of armaments; "a free, open-minded, and absolutely impartial adjustment of all colonial claims." Next came specific guarantees of self-government of national groups within the collapsing Ottoman, Russian, and Austro-Hungarian empires. The fourteenth point called for "a general association of nations...for the purpose of affording mutual guarantees of political independence and territorial integrity to great and small states alike." Anti-imperialist, pacific, liberal in economics as well as politics, it bespoke Wilson's idealistic wish-list for the postwar world. It was also full of contradictions with regard to overlapping national self-determinations and a too-generous estimate of what the other victorious great powers would agree to. Nonetheless, when the peace conference opened in Paris in January 1919, Wilson's Fourteen Points became the framework of the peace treaty.

Wilson appeared personally at the conference and stayed until mid-February to ensure that the fourteenth point, in the form of the Covenant of the League of Nations, was part of the treaty. He then went home for a month. Opposition to the covenant surfaced in the Senate. Although the Democrats' majorities in Congress disappeared in the 1918 election, Wilson returned to Paris and the conference—without a single prominent Republican in his entourage, a huge political mistake. He came home in early July, carrying the Versailles Treaty with the League Covenant embedded in it.

Now it was up to the Senate to ratify, revise, or reject. Senators divided into four factions: supportive Democrats; fourteen "irreconcilables" (twelve of them Republicans) who would not vote for the treaty under any circumstances; strong "reservationists," who wanted serious changes and assurances that American sovereignty was not at risk; and moderate "reservationists," whose quibbles were relatively minor. Wilson, however, refused to consider any changes at all. To rally public opinion, he left on a whistle-stop railroad tour, traveling 8,000 miles in twenty-two days. At Pueblo, Colorado, he broke down from exhaustion. His train sped back to Washington, and there he had a crippling stroke on October 2. Stubborn before, Wilson was unshakeable now, accepting no changes or "reservations" whatever. The extremes—the loyal Senate Democrats and the irreconcilables—defeated the amended treaty on November 19, 38 in favor, 53 against. The public, which welcomed the League, reacted with shock, and forced a reconsideration in March 1920. Although twenty-one Democratic senators voted this time with the reservationists, the necessary two-thirds majority failed to materialize.

In the meantime, 1919 had passed, an annus horribilis. Demobilization of the troops, war industries, and war agencies had been too rapid and disorganized. Consumer prices soared. The railroads, nationalized for the duration, were given back to corporate ownership. In early 1920, the Esch-Cummins Act encouraged cooperation among managements, thus reversing the anti-trust, anti-merger policies in effect since Theodore Roosevelt broke up the Morgan-Harriman Northern Securities combine in 1904. With wartime restraint gone, labor-capital trouble erupted. More than 4,000,000 workers went on strike during 1919. In Seattle a "general strike" of 60,000 workers, lasting five days, demonstrated the power of unions, but also terrified the public, already scared that Bolsheviks and anarchists were taking over the country. In September, 360,000 steel workers began a four-month strike. It ultimately failed, and the steel companies kept out unions until the late 1930s.

Over two dozen race riots broke out around the country, the worst on one of Chicago's lakefront beaches in July when an African American boy drifted into a whites-only area. Before it was over thirty-eight persons were dead and more than five hundred injured. Finally, beginning in November, armed with the Espionage, Sedition, and new Immigration laws, the Department of Justice under Attorney General A. Mitchell Palmer began rounding up immigrants and others suspected of subversive tendencies. The "Palmer Raids" arrested over ten thousand people by the time they ended in mid-1920. More than five hundred were deported.

Only one Progressive measure remained, but it was major: legalizing the vote for women. By 1912 eight states had passed woman suffrage laws, and Roosevelt included it in his Bull Moose platform. Suffragists marched, but Wilson, partly because of his roots and "base" in the socially conservative South and partly from his own inclination, declined to support them. Pressure built, however, during the high tide of Progressivism.

In January 1918 Wilson finally agreed to back a constitutional amendment for woman suffrage. It immediately passed the House of Representatives. It stalled in the Senate, however, and when a vote finally came in October, the amendment was defeated by three votes. Pro-suffrage pressure groups then targeted naysayers in the November election. In the spring, Congress passed the suffrage amendment handily—by 304 to 89 in the House on May 21, 1919, and by 56 to 25 in the Senate on June 4. Though several states (chiefly Southern) rejected it, the necessary thirty-six state legislatures ratified it by August 1920 and the Nineteenth Amendment entered the Constitution. It guaranteed that "The right of citizens of the United States to vote shall not be denied or abridged by the United States or by any State on account of sex." Thus, in 1920, the last of the four "progressive" amendments entered the Constitution.

The Progressive agenda explicated by Bryan, Roosevelt, Wilson, and La Follette was now exhausted. Reform was not, nor were revisions to industrial capitalism, but they needed a few years of breathing space. The Progressive urge, Progressive faith (damaged in many ways by the events of 1919), and Progressive leadership, needed to take a deep breath. The "big four" national leaders all passed from the scene, actually or effectively, around that time. Roosevelt, just sixty-one, died that year. La Follette remained in the Senate but with relatively minor committee duties; he ran for president in 1924 on a "Progressive" ticket but won fewer than 5,000,000 popular and only 13 electoral votes, far behind the Republican winner, Calvin Coolidge. Bryan, although forever popular in the South and West, never held office again after he resigned in 1915 as secretary of state. Wilson, following his stroke in October 1919, remained incapacitated and virtually inactive until he left office in March 1921. Until then, he was in the care of his protective wife Edith, who for months effectively ran the executive branch. Replacing the four great Progressives were conservative presidents Warren G. Harding (1921–23), Calvin Coolidge (1923–29), and Herbert Hoover (1929–33).

To cap all of the political and social ills of 1918–1919, an enormous natural disaster also struck the country. The war was bad enough; 4,700,000 men and women served in the armed forces, 53 percent of them overseas. Of them, over 50,000 were killed in combat, and another 63,000 died from other causes. Much worse, the natural disaster—the great influenza pandemic of 1918–1919—killed about 600,000 Americans and anywhere from 50,000,000 to 100,000,000 people around the world.

The pandemic struck the United States in three waves. In March 1918, at a hastily built army training camp in Kansas called Camp Funston, several hundred new recruits suddenly came down with flu symptoms. A week later, reports of the flu surfaced in New York. This first wave subsided over the summer. But in late August a second wave began with a vengeance at Fort Devens, Massachusetts, a staging ground for shipping out soldiers to France. Hundreds came down with the disease, dozens died in a single day, and the Surgeon General reported that "the dead are stacked about the morgue like cordwood." Troop transports carried sick soldiers, and the disease, to Europe. Initial accusations that the Germans had started the epidemic as biological warfare subsided when it became known that they themselves were being cut down as swiftly as the Allies.

The flu raced across Europe. The Spanish press reported more deaths than elsewhere, only because Spain, a neutral country, was not under military censorship. For this honesty the Spanish were rewarded when the disease was named the "Spanish influenza." It had started, however, in Kansas, possibly as a mutant in chickens or other birds that had passed directly to the young soldiers. Influenza is usually most dangerous among children and the elderly, but this type attacked young persons, possibly because their immune systems reacted to it so vigorously. Lungs filled with fluid, effectively drowning the victims. Not everyone who caught it died, but the case-specific mortality rate was exceptionally high because the disease was more virulent than any normal strain. The cause was a virus and, in an age where microscopy and medicine were still practically innocent of any knowledge of viruses, treatments and cures were ineffective and off the mark.

The second wave took its heaviest toll in the fall of 1918. October was the worst month, with 195,000 reported cases breaking out from San Francisco to Boston. Citizens were warned to avoid public gatherings; movie theaters, schools, and churches closed; face masks were widely distributed and in some towns required. Victory celebrations on Armistice Day, November 11, brought out cheering crowds—and the disease surged again. It abated in December and into January, but a third wave hit in the late winter of 1919. By late spring the flu waned and disappeared as mysteriously as it had started, having burned through the susceptible population, in the United States and around the world. The global death toll from the flu epidemic was much higher than combat-related deaths from the World War itself.

The early spread of the disease was almost certainly faster because of its start in army barracks, jumping then to troop transports and across Europe's battlefields. The absence of scientific knowledge of viruses produced many futile attempts at prevention, though the obvious fact that it was contagious correctly encouraged public authorities to minimize human contacts as best they could.

Public health, sewerage and sanitation, the reduction of parasitic diseases such as hookworm, and improvements in medical and biological sciences in general, were accomplishments of the Progressive era. Cleanliness was a major object of municipal housekeeping reformers, who proved successful and helped the American people emerge much cleaner and longer-lived than at the turn of the century. The flu epidemic demonstrated that research and treatment still had a long way to go. So did other of the Progressives' projects. Inequalities of wealth and income were yawningly wide and had scarcely been reversed despite the graduated income tax. Capital-labor relations were still dangerously bad, revealed by the many strikes of 1919 and the refusal of managements and the courts to accede to collective bargaining. The right to vote had been extended to white women, but denied to black men (and women) by Progressive-era Jim Crow laws in the South, reversing the suffrage promises of Reconstruction. (Black women outside the South, however, now could vote.) The "problem" of immigration was being solved by restricting it. Both men and women Progressives knew profoundly that there was surely more to be done to solve society's problems; but for over a decade, reform was rare; conservative government had returned.

Chapter 6
Ebb tide, 1919–1921

The hope-deflating events of 1919 were augmented by downturns in the economy. The gross national product peaked in constant dollars in 1918, slipped in 1919 and 1920, and fell sharply in 1921. Wartime price inflation of consumer goods continued to rise in 1919, while wages and earnings stagnated. The consumer price index for food and clothing doubled between 1915 and 1920. The prices that farmers received for a bushel of corn or a pound of cotton, highest in 1918–1919, dropped by more than half in 1920. The sharp postwar recession did not fully bottom out until 1921–1922, yet 1919–1920 were hard, uncertain years too.

Farming was about to begin a historic shakeout, though the political strength of agrarians remained sporadically potent through much of the 1920s despite the depletion of Democratic members of Congress. On the Great Plains and farther west, would-be new farmers resumed filing fresh homestead entries in 1919 and 1920 at roughly prewar levels, but the number of final, "proved up" deeds slipped sharply through the decade from almost 8,000,000 acres in 1920 to less than 2,000,000 in 1930. Agriculture as a sector in the economy continued to grow, mainly from increases in the size and capitalization of farms. This meant that small farmers, "homesteaders" in either the technical or the vernacular sense, began to be squeezed out. There were several reasons why: the sharp decline in commodity prices and therefore farmers' income in 1920; competition from larger farms better positioned to buy and use tractors and other new (and expensive) machinery; and the implacable environmental fact that the homesteading frontier had reached the high plains, western North Dakota and Texas, eastern Wyoming and Montana, where lack of rainfall or groundwater made crop raising undependable and risky.

Yet the agrarian dream lived on, enticing young families to go west. Farm people still constituted 30 percent of Americans. As if to ratify the stabilizing of agriculture, the 1920 census revealed that people living in country villages with fewer than 2,500 inhabitants, together with farm folks, no longer were a majority of the American population. City dwellers—admittedly by that generous Census Bureau definition of 2,500 or more residents in an incorporated place—had become a slight majority. The heavily agrarian Congress, for the only time in history, was shocked and refused to redistrict the House of Representatives on the basis of the 1920 census, as constitutionally required (which was a major reason for the agrarians' continued strength in the 1920s).

They were, however, no longer as Democratic as in 1911–1919. Republicans captured the presidency handily in 1920 with 16,100,000 or 60.3 percent of the popular vote for the Harding-Coolidge ticket, to 9,100,000 or a miserable 34.1 percent for the Democrats' James M. Cox and Franklin D. Roosevelt. The electoral vote margin was even wider—404 to 127. Cox and Roosevelt captured only the "Solid South" and Kentucky. The election also brought a Republican landslide in Congress, swelling their majorities in both the Senate (59 to 37) and the House of Representatives (302 to 131 and 2 independents).

The 1920 election thereby intensified the serious shift to the Republicans. The Democrats' high-water mark had been 291 House seats in 1912; they sank to 131 in 1920. Except for the Solid South, which they held, their losses were intersectional—West, Midwest, and East. Comparing the 1920 results with those of 1912, the Democrats lost 10 seats in New Jersey, 11 each in Missouri and Pennsylvania, all 13 of Indiana's, 17 in Illinois, 19 in Ohio, and 22 in New York, with single-digit losses in 18 other states. Democratic majorities in Congress had been crucial for the passage of New-Freedom legislation. Republican majorities in 1918 and their even stronger showing in 1920 ended any chance of further reform legislation, except for the woman suffrage amendment to the Constitution. The most significant laws passed by the Congress elected in 1920 were the Johnson Act of May 19, 1921, restricting immigration on the racist basis of national origins; increased tariff rates, returning the tariff to pre-1913 levels; and the Revenue Act of 1921, which lowered income tax rates from wartime heights (though not to prewar levels; the base rate became 8 percent with a maximum surtax of 50 percent on incomes above $200,000). As far as federal activity was concerned—from the presidency, Congress, or the courts— Progressivism was dead.

As the 1920 election clearly showed, the people were no longer moved by activism in their name. The Progressive battle cry of "the people versus the interests" no longer resonated. The popular mood was resentful, repressive, and disillusioned. The war ended with victory in November 1918, but more than 100,000 Americans had died. The flu epidemic, the "natural disaster" that baffled every person and institution that tried to stop it, killed five or six times more.

The high hopes, stirring rhetoric, and idealism surrounding Wilson's Fourteen Points and the League of Nations had become completely tarnished, not least from the president's own disability and stubbornness. Farmers were squeezed by the double blows of falling prices and rising costs. Industrial workers saw wages fail to rise to meet inflation. Recession set in.

Race relations, never a bright spot among Progressives even in their best days, worsened. A decade earlier, white and black

Progressives had united to establish the National Association for the Advancement of Colored People, and the National Urban League was founded soon after. But these landmark efforts at racial justice struggled in their early years. Wilson segregated the federal bureaucracy more thoroughly than ever, and he showed D. W. Griffith's infamous film, *Birth of a Nation*, which celebrated the Ku Klux Klan of Reconstruction days, in the White House. A reborn KKK emerged on the heels of the film. Between 1920 and 1925 it gained a membership of several million, proclaiming itself "100 percent American." Burning crosses and terrorizing blacks in the South, the Klan became politically powerful across the region. Moreover, it infected northern states too, becoming dominant for a few years in Indiana and Oregon, targeting not only blacks but also Jews, Catholics, and immigrants.

The powerful reform impulses that had coalesced into Progressivism before World War I took a sour turn after 1919 toward conformity, hyperpatriotism, and righteousness. Instead of efforts to democratize governments, broaden the suffrage, and establish industrial and social justice, an apparent majority across the country now applauded business, including large corporations, while the gap in wealth and income among the classes widened. Business had not been so glorified, and its behavior so approved of, since the days of McKinley.

Such was the situation regarding the national mood and in federal legislation—the former, conservative rather than Progressive; the latter, no longer innovative and in important respects, like immigration, downright nativist. But national mood and law making were never the entire Progressive story. The urban-based sides of Progressivism remained, even flourished through the 1920s. The settlement houses continued their educational and social work among the native-born and immigrant urban poor. Social-science research became more institutionalized by the creation of nongovernmental bodies like the National Bureau of Economic Research, the Brookings Institution, the Social Science

Research Council, and others. Philanthropy funded more country schools and public-health clinics in the South. Local and state laws requiring children to attend school to a certain age became regularized. The city-manager form of urban government, a device to promote efficiency and suppress corruption, spread around the country. In these and other ways, less spectacular than some of the pre-1918 changes yet significant, continued through the 1920s and could not have happened without the earlier Progressive activity. While the federal government turned conservative, the social-justice, educational, and local-government Progressives—a great many of them women—found plenty to do. They presented issues and accomplished changes that gained momentum as the urban component of the population rose during the 1920s—almost all population growth in the United States since 1920 has been urban or metropolitan, no longer rural—and they were, in that way, a prelude to the New Deal reforms of the 1930s.

What had Progressivism achieved, when all was said and done? Quite a lot. The United States of 1921 was vastly different from that September day in 1901 when Theodore Roosevelt became president. Great wealth, corporate or individual, had been reined in—by no means fully but to a visible extent. Capped by the income tax amendment, the structure of taxation had been modified, reducing dependence on the tariff, that tax on consumers, and providing much more flexibility for policy making. Local, state, and the federal government had been democratized in major ways—direct election of senators, initiative and referendum laws, woman suffrage, primary elections, and more. Laws limiting the hours that women and children, and in some cases men, could work in a day or a week were on the books, though conservative courts sometimes voided them. Workmen's compensation for on-the-job accidents had become widely accepted. Poverty and endemic diseases had become unacceptable, attacked by settlement houses, social workers, and nongovernmental philanthropy such as the Rockefeller funds. Social scientists provided solid research on social and economic conditions, and the first think tanks were founded in those years. Progress had indeed been achieved on many fronts.

But gaps remained. Progressives had never been fully in accord on certain things—notably on race, ethnic relations, war, and imperialism. Some reformers—Jane Addams, Chicago's Judge Edward Osgood Brown, W. E. B. DuBois, and other founders of the NAACP—did their best to reduce discrimination. Yet some of the movement's chiefs did little: Roosevelt, a believer to the bone in the notion of Anglo-Saxon superiority, had Booker T. Washington to dinner at the White House yet he refused a fair hearing and dishonorably discharged the black soldiers who had been arrested for rioting in Brownsville, Texas, in 1906. Bryan had tolerant words for most groups and "a certain discomfort with white supremacy," but he seldom protested Jim Crow laws, which would have risked his political strength in the South. Woodrow Wilson, Virginia native and son of Confederate sympathizers, was a flat-out segregationist and racist. The eugenics movement was also part of Progressivism; it promoted involuntary sterilization of the "unfit," including the "feeble-minded," carriers of chronic diseases (especially sexually transmitted ones), and even prostitutes and paupers. Linked to it were racial theories classifying "Nordics" (and "Anglo-Saxons") as the fittest of humans, superior to "Mediterraneans" and of course to Africans and Asians. Racism ostensibly backed by science permeated Americans' attitudes, from academics to the man (and woman) on the street, through the early twentieth century, and Progressives participated in it and even promoted it.

On imperialism and wars the Progressives were clearly split. In those days, Roosevelt had no peer in American public life as an ardent expansionist and colonialist. Wilson declared himself an anti-colonialist and peacemaker, and he supported legislation in 1916 and 1917 granting citizenship to Puerto Ricans and promising eventual independence for the Philippines. But he did not hesitate to send in the Marines when Caribbean republics did not meet his standards or to send American forces into Mexico in attempts to control events there. Bryan opposed American empire building in the Philippines and elsewhere and spent much of his brief time as Wilson's secretary of state negotiating thirty treaties establishing arbitration mechanisms with other countries, before he resigned in principle over Wilson's belligerent second *Lusitania* note. Jane Addams and many progressives outside of government refused to support the declaration of war against Germany in 1917 and bravely remained pacifists during and after, despite threats to their liberty under the Espionage and Sedition acts.

Still, Progressives agreed on many issues, most fundamentally on the conviction that there is such a thing as society and that everyone was a member of it, that a common good affected everyone and should be sought in every available way. In this, their outlook contrasted with the rampant individualism and self-seeking that preceded them in the Gilded Age and that returned in the 1920s (and in the 1990s and 2000s, which have been called "the second Gilded Age" because, especially, of increasingly maldistributed wealth and income). Contrary to the socioeconomic philosophy of the novelist guru Ayn Rand, and her devotees Ronald Reagan, Alan Greenspan, and the 2000-era Right, Progressives were revolted at the idea that "greed is good." They rejected Social Darwinism, the economic survival of "the fittest"—whom they knew were simply the best-advantaged. They denied that markets operate automatically and benignly under "natural laws," as Gilded-Age conservatives and latter-day free-market believers have thought.

Instead the Progressives were instrumentalists—and to many of them the most effective instrument of progress was government, at all levels. In this way they agreed with the Populists who preceded them in the 1890s. This belief nurtured urban liberals like Alfred E. Smith, New York's governor in the 1920s, and the people around him—many of them women and/or Jewish, Irish, or from other recent-immigrant groups. Frances Perkins had led the New York Consumers' League since 1910 and was named to the New York industrial commission by Governor Smith; in 1933 Franklin Roosevelt appointed her Secretary of Labor, the first female cabinet member. Belle Moskowitz went on the New York factory commission in 1910 following the Triangle fire; she became a key aide to Governor Smith. They and other leading Progressive women kept reform alive through the 1920s. It has been said that there was an "Al Smith Revolution" prior to the "Roosevelt Revolution" of the 1930s. Smith, an Irish Catholic, anti-prohibition product of New York City's Tammany Hall machine, did not fit the usual Progressive profile in any of those ways. Yet his administration in New York bridged the years and the mentalities between Progressivism and the New Deal.

Nevertheless, a good many Progressives who survived into the 1920s, especially Republicans or one-time Bull Moosers, could not accept the New Deal because for them it went too far toward statism, across the grain of their deep individualism. But others did become New Dealers, seeking in the very different context of the 1930s Depression to work toward a more just and generous society. Progressivism's original agenda and élan sputtered out by 1920. Yet much had been achieved, not to be rolled back. Not all Progressives were silenced; progress had indeed been made and, in places like Smith's New York State, soldiered on. More was needed, and in the dire Depression following 1929, more would eventually come.

References

Chapter 1

The "scanty fortunes" idea may be found in Tocqueville's *Democracy in America* (Garden City, NY: Anchor Books, 1969), 636–37.

Statistics on U.S. population, economics, and society are most easily found in the *Historical Statistics of the United States: Colonial Times to 1970*. 2 vols. (Washington: Government Printing Office, 1975), or the update, *Historical Statistics of the United States: Earliest Times to the Present*. 5 vols. (New York: Cambridge University Press, 2006).

Chapter 2

Worth Robert Miller's "Building a Populist Coalition in Texas, 1892–1896," appeared in *Journal of Southern History* 74 (May 2008).

Milton Friedman expressed his pro-silver views in "Bimetallism Revisited," *Journal of Economic Perspectives* 4 (autumn 1990): 85–104, and "The Crime of 1873," *Journal of Political Economy* 98 (Dec. 1990): 1159–94.

The quotation from Michael Kazin's *A Godly Hero: The Life of William Jennings Bryan* (New York: Anchor Books, 2007), may be found on xviii–xix.

Chapter 3

As Roosevelt used it, the word "bully" had nothing to do with bullying. It simply meant "outstanding" or "first rate," as in "Bully for you."

The TR biographer referred to is Kathleen Dalton: *Theodore Roosevelt: A Strenuous Life* (New York: Vintage Books, 2004), quoted here from 298, and later from 272.

The Walter Rauschenbusch quotes are from his *Christianity and the Social Crisis* (New York: Macmillan, 1908), 265, 352, 345.

The support of Protestant Social Gospelers and social-justice-minded Catholics for trade unions and the labor movement is perceptively traced in Ken Fones-Wolf, "Religion and Trade Union Politics in the United States, 1880–1920," *International Labor and Working-Class History* 34 (fall 1988): 39–55.

That men as well as women took an active role at Hull-House: from Rima Lunin Schultz, "Hull-House after Jane Addams: Revisiting the Social Settlement as Women's Space: 1889–1935," paper delivered at the Newberry Library Seminar on Women and Gender, Chicago, Dec. 5, 2008.

Robert D. Johnston, *The Radical Middle Class: Populist Democracy and the Question of Capitalism in Progressive Era Portland, Oregon* (Princeton, NJ: Princeton University Press, 2003), details the work of U'Ren and the Oregon System.

Chapter 4

The Frank P. Walsh statement is part of his essay, "Labor's Day," in *American Federationist* (a publication of the American Federation of Labor) 25 (Oct. 1918): 895, 897. Also helpful on the U.S. Industrial Relations Commission are Allen Davis, "The Campaign for the Industrial Relations Commission, 1911–1913," *Mid-America* 45 (Oct. 1963): 211–28; the obituary of Walsh in the *New York Times*, May 3, 1939; and Shelton Stromquist, *Reinventing "The People": The Progressive Movement, The Class Problem, and the Origins of Modern Liberalism* (Urbana: University of Illinois Press, 2006), esp. chap. 7.

The Elizabeth Sanders quotation is in her book, *Roots of Reform: Farmers, Workers, and the American State, 1877–1917* (Chicago: University of Chicago Press, 1999), 169. The later quotation is on 158. Sanders' book articulates the thesis that Progressivism's legislative muscle lay in agrarian parts of the country. Party affiliation—Populist, Democratic, or insurgent Republican— was less important than connections to the agrarian economy and the concentration of political strength in such districts. In urban or mixed districts, she argues, the interests of labor (the natural ally of agrarians) were diluted by competing forces. Close students may want to know that Sanders' interpretation is recent and, to me, convincingly solves the problem of interparty, intersectional, urban *and* rural support for Progressivism. Earlier interpretations such as Robert Wiebe's widely read *The Search for Order* (1967) stress reformers' search for social control of both the new industrial capitalism and the mass of potentially radical people. Others such as Martin Sklar had written in the 1960s, from a Marxist perspective, that Progressive-era reform was a cover for business interests. This became known as the "corporate-liberal" interpretation. In *The Corporate Reconstruction of American Capitalism, 1890-1916* (1988), Sklar explored more subtly and in more detail how capitalism moved "from the competitive to the corporate stage of its development" by 1914.

The Eric Rauchway quotation on Bryanites: in "Armchair Warriors," *Reviews in American History* 32 (2004): 228. For a comprehensive survey of wealth distribution comparing the Gilded Age and Progressivism with the present, see Louis Uchitelle, "The Richest of the Rich, Proud of a New Gilded Age," *New York Times*, July 15, 2007, and supportive letters to the editor, July 17, 2007. One of the few contemporary treatments is Willford Isbell King, *Income in the United States, Its Amount and Distribution, 1909-1919* (New York: Harcourt, Brace and Co., for the National Bureau of Economic Research, 1921-22), 146.

Bryan's speech in Congress, "An Income Tax," given Jan. 30, 1894, may be found in *Speeches of William Jennings Bryan, rev. and arranged by Himself, with a Biographical Introduction by Mary Baird Bryan, His Wife* (New York: Funk & Wagnalls, 1913), I:159-79. Quotations here are from 161, 163-65, and 174.

For E. R. A. Seligman, see his *The Income Tax: A Study of the History, Theory, and Practice of Income Taxation at Home and Abroad* (1911; 2d ed., New York: Macmillan, 1914), 33, 640. The *Hartford Courant* quote appears in John D. Buenker, "The Ratification of the Federal Income Tax Amendment," *Cato Journal* 1 (spring 1981): 221-22.

The Herbert Croly quotations are in *The Promise of American Life* (1909; New York: Macmillan, 1911), at 118-19, 155-57, 381-82, 409. Theodore Roosevelt's Osawatomie speech is available online at www.theodore-roosevelt.com/trnationalismspeech.html.

Biographies of Wilson include H. W. Brands, *Woodrow Wilson* (New York: Times Books, 2003) and John Milton Cooper, *The*

Warrior and the Priest: Woodrow Wilson and Theodore Roosevelt (Cambridge, MA: Belknap Press of Harvard University Press, 1983).

"divided heart on race" of TR: Kathleen Dalton's phrase, in *Theodore Roosevelt: A Strenuous Life*, 92.

Wilson, "ours is a program of liberty," is in Lewis L. Gould, *Four Hats in the Ring: The 1912 Election and the Birth of Modern American Politics* (Lawrence: University of Kansas Press, 2008), 164.
Wilson explained his program in *The New Freedom: A Call for the Emancipation of the Generous Energies of a People* (Garden City, NY: Doubleday, Page, 1913).

The commentator on socialism is David J. O'Brien, "A Vote for Socialism: Like Christianity, It's Never Been Tried." In *Commonweal*, July 18, 2008, 18.

Chapter 6

Bryan's "certain discomfort with white supremacy" are words taken from Kazin, *A Godly Hero*, 227.

Further reading

Some Progressives Speak for Themselves

Croly, Herbert. *The Promise of American Life*. New York: Macmillan, 1909.

Eisenach, Eldon J., ed. *The Social and Political Thought of American Progressivism*. Indianapolis, IN: Hackett Publishing Company, 2006.

James, William. *Pragmatism: A New Name for Some Old Ways of Thinking: Popular Lectures on Philosophy*. New York: Longmans, Green, 1907.

Lloyd, Henry Demarest. *Wealth against Commonwealth*. [1894] Westport, CT: Greenwood Press, 1976.

Lippmann, Walter. *Drift and Mastery: An Attempt to Diagnose the Current Unrest*. New York: Mitchell Kennerley, 1914.

Rauschenbusch, Walter. *Christianity and the Social Crisis*. New York: Macmillan, 1907.

Ross, Edward Alsworth. *Sin and Society: An Analysis of Latter-Day Iniquity*. Boston: Houghton, Mifflin, 1907.

Overviews of the Progressive Era

Diner, Steven J. *A Very Different Age: Americans in the Progressive Era*. New York: Hill & Wang, 1998.

Fink, Leon. *Major Problems in the Gilded Age and Progressive Era*. Lexington, MA: D. C. Heath, 1993.

Flanagan, Maureen. *America Reformed: Progressives and Progressivisms, 1890s–1920s*. New York: Oxford University Press, 2007.

McGerr, Michael. *A Fierce Discontent: The Rise and Fall of the Progressive Movement in America, 1870–1920*. New York: Free Press, 2003.

Sanders, Elizabeth. *Roots of Reform: Farmers, Workers, and the American State 1877–1917*. Chicago: University of Chicago Press, 1999.

Stromquist, Shelton. *Reinventing "The People": The Progressive Movement, The Class Problem, and the Origins of Modern Liberalism*. Urbana: University of Illinois Press, 2006.

Historiography

Johnston, Robert D. "Re-Democratizing the Progressive Era: The Politics of Progressive Era Political Historiography." *Journal of the Gilded Age and Progressive Era* 1 (Jan. 2002): 68–92.

Biographies

Brands, H. W. *Woodrow Wilson*. New York: Times Books, 2003.

Brown, Victoria Bissell. *The Education of Jane Addams*. Philadelphia: University of Pennsylvania Press, 2004.

Dalton, Kathleen. *Theodore Roosevelt: A Strenuous Life*. New York: Vintage Books, 2004.

Davis, Allen F. *American Heroine: The Life and Legend of Jane Addams*. Chicago: Ivan Dee, 2000.

Kazin, Michael. *A Godly Hero: The Life of William Jennings Bryan*. New York: Anchor Books, 2007.

Knight, Louise D. *Citizen: Jane Addams and the Struggle for Democracy*. Chicago: University of Chicago Press, 2005.

Lewis, David Levering. *W. E. B. DuBois: A Biography*. New York: Henry Holt, 2008.

Salvatore, Nick. *Eugene V. Debs: Citizen and Socialist*. Urbana: University of Illinois Press, 2007.

Sklar, Kathryn Kish. *Florence Kelley and the Nation's Work: The Rise of Women's Political Culture, 1830–1900*. New Haven, CT: Yale University Press, 1995.

Unger, Nancy C. *Fighting Bob La Follette: The Righteous Reformer*. Chapel Hill: University of North Carolina Press, 2000.

Weisberger, Bernard A. *La Follettes of Wisconsin: Love and Politics in Progressive America*. Madison: University of Wisconsin Press, 1994.

A Few Specific Topics

Andrews, Thomas G. *Killing for Coal: America's Deadliest Labor War* [the 1914 Colorado coal strike and Ludlow massacre]. Cambridge, MA: Harvard University Press, 2008.

Capozzola, Christopher J. N., *Uncle Sam Wants You: World War I and the Making of the Modern American Citizen.* New York: Oxford University Press, 2008.

Deverell, William, and Tom Sitton, eds. *California Progressivism Revisited.* Berkeley: University of California Press, 1994.

Flamming, Douglas. *Bound for Freedom: Black Los Angeles in Jim Crow America.* Berkeley: University of California Press, 2005.

Flanagan, Maureen. *Seeing with Their Hearts: Chicago Women and the Vision of the Good City, 1871–1933.* Princeton, NJ: Princeton University Press, 2002.

Gordon, Linda. *The Great Arizona Orphan Abduction.* Cambridge, MA: Harvard University Press, 1999.

Greene, Julie. *The Canal Builders: Making America's Empire at the Panama Canal.* New York: Penguin Press, 2009.

Gregory, James N. *Southern Diaspora: How the Great Migrations of Black and White Southerners Transformed America.* Chapel Hill: University of North Carolina Press, 2005.

Grossman, James R. *Land of Hope: Chicago, Black Southerners, and the Great Migration.* Chicago: University of Chicago Press, 1989.

Higham, John. *Strangers in the Land: Patterns of American Nativism, 1860–1925.* New Brunswick, NJ: Rutgers University Press, 2002.

Johnston, Robert D. *The Radical Middle Class: Populist Democracy and the Question of Capitalism in Progressive Era Portland, Oregon.* Princeton: Princeton University Press, 2003.

Kazin, Michael. *Barons of Labor: The San Francisco Building Trades and Union Power in the Progressive Era.* Urbana: University of Illinois Press, 1987.

Kloppenberg, James T. *Uncertain Victory: Social Democracy and Progressivism in European and American Thought, 1870–1920.* New York: Oxford University Press, 1986.

McMath, Robert C. *American Populism: A Social History, 1877–1898.* New York: Hill & Wang, 1993.

Postel, Charles. *The Populist Vision.* New York: Oxford University Press, 2007.

Sugrue, Thomas J. *Sweet Land of Liberty: The Forgotten Struggle for Civil Rights in the North.* New York: Random House, 2008.

Index

Y